T0113078

Sip and Sensibility

Sip and Sensibility

13-Digit ISBN: 978-1-40034-399-7
10-Digit ISBN: 1-40034-399-2

This book may be ordered by mail from the publisher. Please include $5.99 for postage and handling. Please support your local bookseller first!

Books published by Cider Mill Press Book Publishers are available at special discounts for bulk purchases in the United States by corporations, institutions, and other organizations. For more information, please contact the publisher.

Cider Mill Press Book Publishers
"Where Good Books Are Ready for Press"
501 Nelson Place
Nashville, Tennessee 37214

cidermillpress.com

Typography: Dico Typewriter, Evalfey Variable, Warnock Pro

Printed in Malaysia

24 25 26 27 28 OFF 5 4 3 2 1
First Edition

Sip and Sensibility

An Inspired Literary Cocktail Collection

TIM RAYBORN

Illustrations by Adèle Leyris

Contents

Introduction

Cocktails and mixed drinks have been a part of drinking culture for a long time. Not content merely to ferment beverages on their own, people have been blending various spirits with other ingredients, probably all the way back to the beginning of civilization. In earlier times, such mixes were often used as medicines, being combinations of alcohol with various herbs, spices, and so on. These were not necessarily meant to be enjoyed on an everyday basis, but had specific uses. Indeed, some early medical texts warn about taking these curatives if you don't really need to!

But that probably didn't stop anyone from trying out their own blends at home, assuming they could get their hands on the ingredients. The mixing of alcoholic drinks with other alcoholic drinks, or with nonalcoholic beverages, seems to have taken hold in Europe by the sixteenth century, but it could well have started much earlier. By the nineteenth century, the imbibing of mixed drinks was all the rage, at least in certain circles. Writers of all kinds loved penning odes to their favorite concoctions, or at least including them in their tales, so that their characters could enjoy them, too. And many of these works became classics of modern literature.

In case you're wondering, the word "cocktail" has several possible origins:

It might come from a mispronunciation of coquetier, the French word for eggcup. In New Orleans, an eighteenth-century apothecary named Antoine Amédée Peychaud, who invented his own bitters, was said to have served said bitters with brandy in an eggcup. Customers would drink his "cocktays" for their health.

Or, it might come from the practice of tavern owners mixing the leftovers and dregs (called the tailings) of their barrels into one (possibly unpleasant) drink. They would then sell these mixed drinks, maybe at a discount. The taps of the barrels were sometimes called "cocks." Thus, you would be drinking the tailings from the barrel's cock (no immature laughing, please!).

Also, it might come from the seventeenth-century term cocktail, which described an animal, such as a horse, that had a rooster-like tail. This was mainly true for horses with docked tails, ones used for pulling coaches and such. But racehorses didn't normally have docked tails, so any horses that did have such tails would have stood out on a racetrack because they'd been changed or visibly altered. Given how much horse racing fans like to drink, the theory is that the term entered drinking nomenclature to describe a drink that had been altered, or spruced up. This one seems like a bit of a stretch, it must be said.

Any or none of these theories might be the word's true origin, but regardless, it was already in use by the early nineteenth century and has remained so ever since.

This little book is a compendium of literary references to cocktails and other mixed drinks, beginning in Ancient Egypt and continuing into the twenty-first century. Then there is a shorter section of some of the favorite mixed drinks of well-known authors, things that they might have enjoyed sipping while creating their masterworks. While some of the earliest drinks mentioned are not "true" cocktails as we think of them today, they show that the concept of mixing various ingredients with alcohol goes back a very long way. There are recipes for each drink, so that you can try them out, if you wish.

But always remember: it's a sad reality that many authors drank entirely too much alcohol, drastically dimming their brilliance and cutting their lives tragically short because of their dependence on liquid inspiration. It should go without saying that while these classic and not-so-familiar recipes might be enticing, please drink responsibly and in moderation.

In the vast expanse of the world's literature, there is a wealth of literary references to drinks of all kinds, and this book supplies only a short introduction to them. Perhaps it will also inspire you to seek out some of these masterpieces, and maybe enjoy reading them with a good mixed drink.

The Ancient & Early Modern World

The ancient world didn't have cocktails per se, but people all around the Mediterranean were fond of drinking wine and other beverages with other ingredients added in: sugar, honey, herbs, spices, and so on. And, as we've noted, these early mixed drinks were just as often drunk for medicinal purposes as they were for enjoyment, either with food or on their own. Sometimes people were advised not to drink too much if they had no ailments! But for the modern drinker, any of these should be perfectly enjoyable. They would also be excellent options for parties and other celebrations, especially if you're going for a specific theme.

Wine Infused with Mint, Thyme & Sage

From the Tomb of Scorpion I, c. 3150 BCE

5 fresh mint leaves

3 fresh sage leaves

2 sprigs of fresh thyme

1 part wine

Place the herbs and wine in a mixing glass and muddle.

Let the mixture steep for 1 to 2 hours at room temperature for a quick infusion, or refrigerate for anywhere from 4 hours to overnight.

Strain into a Nick & Nora glass and drink within 2 days.

[Wine is] the blood of those who had once battled against the gods and from whom, when they had fallen and had become commingled with the earth, they believed vines to have sprung.

—Plutarch, Moralia, *first century CE*

Despite that rather gruesome origin story regarding wine, the Egyptian upper classes were fond of the drink, while simple beers were the favored alcohol of the workers and servants. Wine was related to the blood of Osiris, the god of resurrection, and had an important place in Ancient Egyptian religious rituals, as well as in medicines. It seems more often to have been red, though references to white wines do appear at times.

This "recipe" is based on analysis of some jars found inside the "Scorpion King's" tomb, which show remnants of wine infused with herbs, including mint, thyme, and sage. There are other ingredients, but a simple infusion using just these herbs in a white or red wine will produce a lovely and refreshing drink, perfect for a summer's day.

Conditum Paradoxum
(Surprise Wine)

Apicius, Anonymous, fifth century CE

1 (750 ml) bottle of wine

1 cup honey

1 date

1 teaspoon black pepper

½ teaspoon fennel seeds

2 bay leaves

Pinch of saffron threads

Bring 75 ml (about ⅓ cup) of wine and the honey to a boil in a saucepan, stirring often until the honey has emulsified.

Reduce the heat so that the mixture simmers and stir in the remaining honey and the rest of the ingredients. Cover the pan and simmer for 10 minutes.

Strain the mixture into a pitcher through a fine-mesh sieve lined with a coffee filter.

Add the remaining wine to the strained mixture and stir to combine. Serve chilled.

This excellent spiced wine.

Apicius is a book of cookery of all kinds, remarkable for its age. The author is anonymous, though that hasn't stopped people from guessing who it might have been. It's possible that some form of the book was written in the first century, though the surviving version seems to date from the fifth century.

This wine would be perfect for a celebration, such as Saturnalia (the big Roman holiday in December). Red or white wine will work for this recipe, though white might be preferable, since it is best chilled, and white was the most common wine drunk in Roman times.

Rose Petal Wine

Apicius, Anonymous, fifth century CE

---

1 (750 ml) bottle of wine

1½ cups rose petals, plus more for garnish

Honey, to taste

Pour the wine into a large pitcher.

Place one-third of the rose petals on a piece of cheesecloth.

Tie the cheesecloth closed and submerge it in the wine. Let the mixture steep in the refrigerator for a week.

After the week has passed, remove the sachet from the wine and repeat Steps 2 and 3 with another one-third of the rose petals.

Repeat Step 4 and then repeat Steps 2 and 3 with the remaining rose petals.

Remove the sachet from the wine, stir in honey to taste, and garnish each serving with additional rose petals.

Another delicious and very simple mix from the *Apicius* manuscript, this Roman serve is not a modern rosé, but rather wine literally infused with rose petals. The recipe is simple and again would likely work better with a dry white wine. You can sweeten the wine to taste with sugar or honey (as indicated in the original instructions), or leave it dry to let the flavors of the rose petals really come through.

Piment (Spiced White Wine)

Perceval, the Story of the Grail
Written by Chrétien de Troyes, late twelfth century

1 (750 ml) bottle of dry white wine

Fresh herbs of your choosing

Combine the wine and herbs in a saucepan and bring to a boil.

Reduce the heat and simmer for 5 minutes.

Remove the pan from heat and let the wine cool completely.

Pour each individual serving into a cocktail shaker, fill it two-thirds of the way with ice, and shake until chilled.

Strain into a Champagne flute or coupe and enjoy.

And spiced wine they drank; piment,
Without sweet honey or pepper blent;

Descriptions of banquets in medieval texts can be lengthy, depicting every sumptuous dish in detail. This late twelfth-century French poem is no exception, though it's mainly concerned with the quest for the Holy Grail, that most famous of objects from the King Arthur tales. Here, we have a fantastic feast accompanied by a spiced wine known as piment, a preparation that probably dates back to Ancient Rome. The poem here tells us that this particular piment was not blended with honey or black pepper, meaning that other spices were used. White or red wine was used to make piment; this recipe calls for a dry white wine.

Hippocras
(Mulled Red Wine)

This Is the Boke of Cokery
Anonymous, printed by Richard Pynson, 1500

---

4 cups red wine
1 oz. cinnamon sticks
½ oz. fresh ginger, chopped
¼ oz. grains of paradise
¼ oz. long pepper
½ lb. sugar

Place all of the ingredients in a large pitcher or container, cover it, and chill it in the refrigerator for 4 or more hours.

When ready to serve, strain the mixture into a clean pitcher. Add ice, stir until chilled, and enjoy.

To a quart of red wine, add an ounce of cinnamon and half an ounce of ginger; a quarter of an ounce of grains of paradise and long pepper, and half a pound of sugar. Bruise all this, not too small, and strain the wine through a cloth bag.

Now, cookbooks aren't exactly "literature," but they are plentiful in England and beyond from the fourteenth century onward, and they provide a fascinating glimpse into the foods of the upper classes (and sometimes more commonly eaten foods, as well), some of which look very tasty, while other might leave your stomach churning. Recipes for spiced wine are common in these collections. Hippocras (one of its many spellings) is basically a mulled red wine with sugar, cinnamon, and other delectable ingredients. The recipe given in the book is easy to follow and many modern historical cookery experts have used its example to fashion their own versions.

Lamb's Wool

The Diary of Samuel Pepys, Samuel Pepys, 1659-69

1 part ale

1 cup sugar

1 part roasted apple pulp

Dash of nutmeg

Place the ale and sugar in a glass and stir to combine.

Pour the roasted apple pulp on top of the cocktail, top with a dusting of nutmeg, and stir to combine.

We got well home... Being come home, we to cards, till two in the morning, and drinking lamb's-wool [A beverage consisting of ale mixed with sugar, nutmeg, and the pulp of roasted apples]. November 9th, 1666

The Diary of Samuel Pepys offers a fascinating glimpse into daily life in mid-seventeenth century England, during the Restoration of the monarchy, when King Charles II was on the throne. This entry describes a rather harrowing evening, when Pepys and his friends witnessed a fire that, luckily, was put out. It had only been a few months since a terrible fire had ravaged much of London, so no doubt they were thankful, and after getting home, they partook of this comforting beverage and cards to relax.

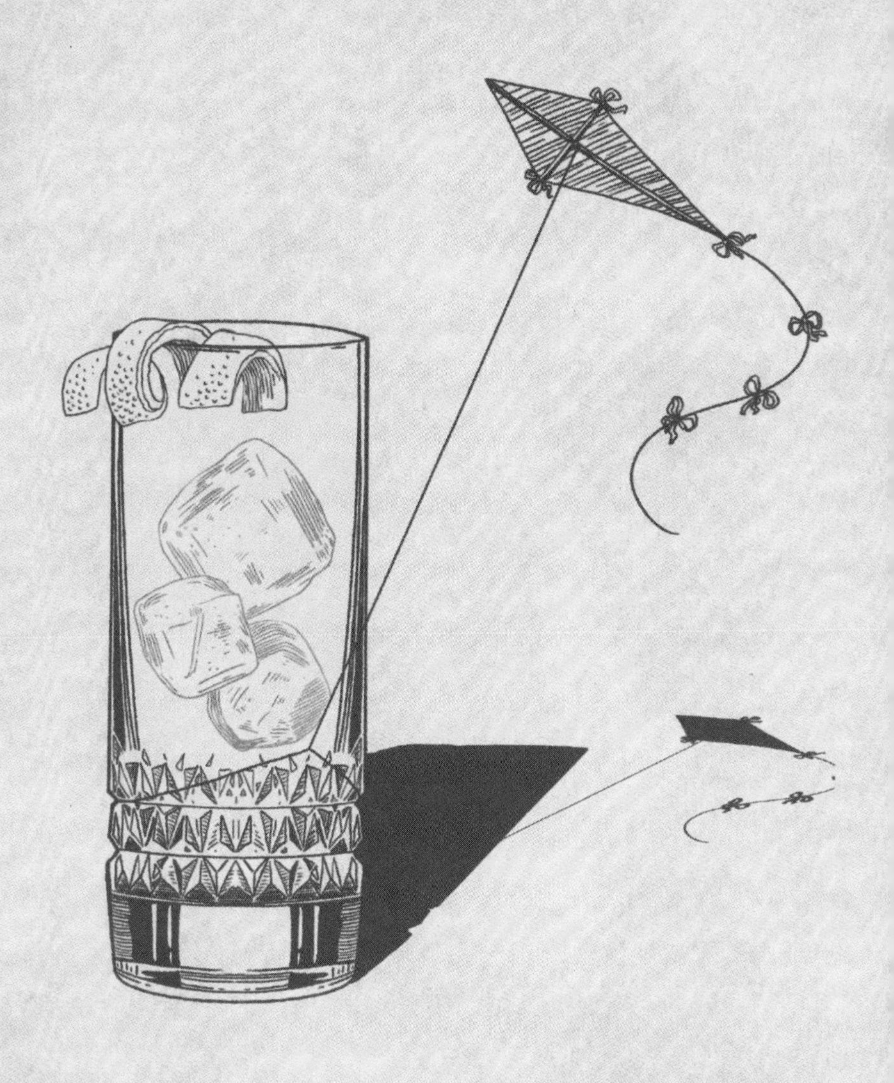

The Nineteenth Century

The nineteenth century was the time when mixed drinks began to come into their own as beverages enjoyable in their own right, without having to use the excuse of "medicinal purposes" to justify one's favorite evening tipple. Mentions of mixed drinks start to show up in a lot of novels and short stories, too. Here is a generous sampling of mixed drinks and literary works you might not know, but are worthy of your time.

Stone-Fence

A History of New York, Washington Irving, 1809

---

8 cups apple cider

4 cups bourbon

5 cinnamon sticks

3 orange peels

30 to 40 whole cloves

Place the apple cider, bourbon, and cinnamon sticks in a slow cooker and cook on low for 2 hours, making sure the mixture does not come to a boil.

Cut the orange peels into rectangles and press the cloves into them.

Garnish each serving of the cocktail with a clove-studded square of orange peel and enjoy.

They lay claim to be the first inventors of those recondite beverages, cock-tail, stone-fence, and sherry-cobbler.

In this passage, Irving's satirical work makes fun of the colonists of Maryland, or "Merryland," claiming that they were always making merry with alcohol, hence the name. And if they were the first to produce these cocktails, as Irving claims, no wonder they were making merry! In addition, he says: "They were, moreover, great horse-racers and cock-fighters, mighty wrestlers and jumpers, and enormous consumers of hoe-cake and bacon."

The Stone-Fence is most commonly a mixture of apple cider with spirits (usually bourbon, brandy, or rum), and a dash of bitters. It was apparently enjoyed in colonial America and makes a great autumnal cocktail. Wrestling and jumping are optional.

Negus

Mansfield Park, Jane Austen, 1814

1 oz. spiced port

½ oz. fresh lemon juice

½ cup boiling water

1 lemon slice, for garnish

Place the spiced port and lemon juice in a mug, pour the boiling water over the mixture, and stir to combine.

Garnish with the slice of lemon and enjoy.

[Fanny stopped] to view the happy scene, and take a last look at the five or six determined couples who were still hard at work; and then, creeping slowly up the principal staircase, pursued by the ceaseless country-dance, feverish with hopes and fears, soup and negus, sore-footed and fatigued, restless and agitated, yet feeling, in spite of everything, that a ball was indeed delightful.

At a grand ball, the novel's heroine, Frances "Fanny" Price had been urged by Sir Thomas Bertram to retire for the evening, but she stops to behold the last of the revelers, with their aching limbs, apparently "feverish" with negus, among other things.

But what is negus? It's a spiced port that was all the rage in Regency England and later. Mixed with hot water, oranges and lemons, spices, and sometimes sugar (though the port was probably sweet enough!), it must have packed a bit of a "punch" (pun intended) to keep those weary dancers pressing on into the evening!

Gin Twist

Saint Ronan's Well, Sir Walter Scott, 1823

1 part gin
1 part fresh lemon juice
Splash of simple syrup
2 parts boiling water

Place the gin, lemon juice, and simple syrup in a mug and pour the boiling water over the mixture.

Stir to combine and enjoy.

"Then," said the Captain, "Sir Binco, I will beg the favour of your company to the smoking room, where we may have a cigar and a glass of gin-twist; and we will consider how the honour of the company must be supported and upholden upon the present conjuncture."

The smoking room, or other such suitable chamber, was a time-honored place in the nineteenth century, where the men-folk could go and discuss weighty matters of the world, most often with smoking and alcohol. Brandy, Scotch, and many other drinks were on offer, though in this case, the drink of choice is the Gin Twist. This classic cocktail blends gin, lemon juice, syrup, and hot water into a warming drink that would be welcome on chilly nights. Cigars and insufferable discussions of current affairs not required.

Pineapple Rum

The Pickwick Papers, Charles Dickens, 1838

1 part rum

1 part pineapple juice

10 fresh mint leaves

1 pineapple slice, for garnish

Place the rum, pineapple juice, and mint in a mason jar filled with ice and stir until chilled.

Garnish with the pineapple slice and enjoy.

Beside him stood a glass of reeking hot pine-apple rum-and-water, with a slice of lemon in it; and every time the red-nosed man stopped to bring the round of toast to his eye, with the view of ascertaining how it got on, he imbibed a drop or two of the hot pine-apple rum-and-water, and smiled upon the rather stout lady, as she blew the fire.

Sam Weller, devoted friend to Samuel Pickwick, is calling at an inn, The Marquis of Granby, to visit his father and mother-in-law. There, he spots one Mr. Stiggins, who makes quite the spectacle of himself: "He was a prim-faced, red-nosed man, with a long, thin countenance, and a semi-rattlesnake sort of eye—rather sharp, but decidedly bad. He wore very short trousers, and black cotton stockings, which, like the rest of his apparel, were particularly rusty. His looks were starched, but his white neckerchief was not, and its long limp ends straggled over his closely buttoned waistcoat in a very uncouth and unpicturesque fashion."

In any case, he is quite fond of pineapple rum, which as the name implies, is a blend of rum and pineapple juice, sometimes with other herbs such as mint, or spices such as nutmeg. In Dickens' time, it might have been served hot, but it can also be served cold for a refreshing summer drink.

Rum Toddy

Martin Chuzzlewit, Charles Dickens, 1838

1 oz. rum

1 tablespoon honey

2 teaspoons fresh lemon juice

½ cup boiling water

1 lemon slice, for garnish

1 cinnamon stick, for garnish

Place the rum, honey, and lemon juice in a mug, pour the boiling water over the mixture, and stir to combine.

Garnish with the slice of lemon and enjoy.

He could hang about a bar-room, discussing the affairs of the nation, for twelve hours together; and in that time could hold forth with more intolerable dulness, chew more tobacco, smoke more tobacco, drink more rum-toddy... than any private gentleman of his acquaintance.

Major Pawkins ("a gentleman of Pennsylvanian origin") has a potential political career in the United States ahead of him, but due to some unwise financial decisions, "Mrs Pawkins kept a boarding-house, and Major Pawkins rather 'loafed' his time away than otherwise." No matter, the major is fond of the Rum Toddy, a classic drink with rum, hot water, lemon juice, honey, and spices, which no doubt helps while away the hours while he discusses important affairs of the day ... and his wife does all the real work. Thankfully, you can enjoy a Rum Toddy today without worrying about whether doing so is causing someone else to suffer from an unfair distribution of labor.

Smoking Bishop

A Christmas Carol, Charles Dickens, 1843

1 (750 ml) bottle of red wine

1 tablespoon orange zest

1 tablespoon lemon zest

3 whole cloves

1 star anise pod

2 cardamom pods

½ cup honey

½ cup ruby port

Cinnamon sticks, for garnish

Place all of the ingredients, except for the port and cinnamon sticks, in a saucepan and bring to a simmer.

Remove the pan from heat, stir in the port, and ladle the cocktail into mugs. Garnish each serving with a cinnamon stick and enjoy.

"A merrier Christmas, Bob, my good fellow, than I have given you, for many a year! I'll raise your salary, and endeavour to assist your struggling family, and we will discuss your affairs this very afternoon, over a Christmas bowl of smoking bishop, Bob! Make up the fires, and buy another coal-scuttle before you dot another I, Bob Cratchit!"

After the grouchy old miser, Ebeneezer Scrooge, has his ghost-driven change of heart on Christmas Eve, he invites his put-upon clerk to sit with him on a cold December afternoon by a warm fire and discuss Bob's new salary and other assistance over a "Christmas bowl of smoking bishop."

This warming winter drink would have been the perfect concoction on such a chilly day. It's a delicious combination of red wine (a Burgundy would be perfect), ruby port, sugar, spices, and citrus fruits, all warmed so that it gently steams (hence, the "smoking" part of the name). It might just ward off a few of those unwanted Christmas spirits—you know, the paranormal kind...

Rum & Lemon Punch

David Copperfield, Charles Dickens, 1850

½ oz. fresh lemon juice

2 oz. rum

1 lemon twist

Place the lemon juice and lemon twist in a highball glass and fill the glass with ice.

Add the rum, stir to combine, and enjoy.

I informed Mr. Micawber that I relied upon him for a bowl of punch, and led him to the lemons. His recent despondency, not to say despair, was gone in a moment. I never saw a man so thoroughly enjoy himself amid the fragrance of lemon-peel and sugar, the odour of burning rum, and the steam of boiling water, as Mr. Micawber did that afternoon. It was wonderful to see his face shining at us out of a thin cloud of these delicate fumes, as he stirred, and mixed, and tasted, and looked as if he were making, instead of punch, a fortune for his family down to the latest posterity.

Poor Mr. Micawber always finds himself in dire situations with money, yet he somehow remains optimistic that "something is about to turn up." In this case, David Copperfield kindly diverts Micawber's attention away from his latest financial woes and back to the task at hand: the fashioning of a Rum & Lemon Punch! While this particular version is served on the rocks, don't hesitate to put it in a mug and add a bit of boiling water when the weather turns cold.

Champagne Cock-Tail

The Innocents Abroad, Mark Twain, 1869

1 sugar cube

Juice of 1 lemon wedge

1 part Angostura Bitters

2 parts Champagne

1 lemon twist, for garnish

Place the sugar cube in a Champagne flute and squeeze the juice from the lemon wedge over it.

Add the bitters and top with the Champagne.

Garnish with the lemon twist and enjoy.

Our general said, "We will take a whiskey straight."

[A stare from the Frenchman.]

Well, if you don't know what that is, give us a champagne cock-tail."

[A stare and a shrug.]

Twain, along with a group of travelers, are frustrated to discover that when in Paris, an establishment that proclaims "All manner of American drinks artistically prepared here" doesn't have to follow through on that promise. As you'll see, Twain & Co. list a whole selection of popular mixed drinks of the day while trying to find common ground with the inept barkeep.

Of course, "champagne cock-tail" is a very generic term for just about anything mixed with Champagne, so their request was admittedly rather vague. Still, a classic version of the recipe is simply Champagne, Angostura Bitters, a sugar cube, and a lemon or orange twist, a version that has been around since the 1850s, and might well have been what Twain and the others were expecting.

Sherry Cobbler

The Innocents Abroad, Mark Twain, 1869

1 tablespoon caster (superfine) sugar

2 orange slices

3½ oz. Amontillado or Oloroso sherry

1 sprig of fresh mint, for garnish

Place the sugar and orange slices in a cocktail shaker and muddle.

Add ice and the sherry and shake until chilled.

Fill a tin cup with crushed ice and strain the cocktail over it.

Garnish with the mint and enjoy.

"Well, then, give us a sherry cobbler."

Twain and the others try again, but to no avail. The Sherry Cobbler sounds like a dessert, but it's really a simple drink dating from the nineteenth century. It is usually made with dry sherry, citrus, and syrup, served over ice. In any case, by the 1860s it had definitely been around long enough that any respectable bartender should have been expected to be familiar with it.

Brandy Smash

The Innocents Abroad, Mark Twain, 1869

---

5 fresh mint leaves

2 oz. brandy

½ teaspoon simple syrup

Chill a cocktail glass in the freezer.

Place the ingredients in a cocktail shaker, fill it two-thirds of the way with ice, and shake until chilled.

Strain into the chilled cocktail glass and enjoy.

The Frenchman was checkmated. This was all Greek to him.

"Give us a brandy smash!"

By now, the would-be patrons are getting frustrated. The Brandy Smash, also dating from the early to mid-nineteenth century, was a classic mixed drink that should have been available in any bar. It was especially popular during the Civil War era and afterward. Most often made with brandy or cognac, mint leaves, and syrup, it can also be served with or without soda, depending on the drinker's preference.

Eye-Opener

The Innocents Abroad, Mark Twain, 1869

1 teaspoon caster (superfine) sugar

1½ oz. rum

2 dashes of curaçao

2 dashes of apricot brandy

1 egg yolk (optional)

Chill a coupe in the freezer.

Place the sugar, rum, curaçao, and apricot brandy in a cocktail shaker and muddle.

Add ice and the egg yolk, shake vigorously, and strain into the chilled coupe.

The Frenchman began to back away, suspicious of the ominous vigor of the last order—began to back away, shrugging his shoulders and spreading his hands apologetically. The General followed him up and gained a complete victory. The uneducated foreigner could not even furnish a Santa Cruz Punch, an Eye-Opener, a Stone-Fence, or an Earthquake. It was plain that he was a wicked impostor.

It's pretty obvious that our frustrated visitors aren't going to get anything that they want, as Twain rattles off a list of drinks denied to them. Among these names is one called an Eye-Opener, which stands out and makes you wonder just what goes into it (do you really want to know?). The Eye-Opener is eye-opening, to say the least, being a mixture of rum, orange and apricot liqueurs, and an egg yolk. Bear in mind that should you choose to add this ingredient, there are health concerns about consuming raw eggs in any drink. Should you think it not worth the risk, it's also possible to make a perfectly satisfying mixed drink without the egg.

Earthquake

The Innocents Abroad, Mark Twain, 1869

---

1 oz. cognac

1 oz. absinthe

Place the ingredients in a mixing glass, fill it two-thirds of the way with ice, and stir until chilled.

Strain over 3 large ice cubes into a rocks glass and enjoy.

Having spent time in San Francisco a few years prior to his grand European adventure, you might imagine that earthquakes were something Twain would have wanted to avoid. But this Earthquake, or *Tremblement de terre*, appears to be a product of France, all the more reason the bartender should have had an acquaintance with it! To be fair, some sources credit the drink to the painter Henri de Toulouse-Lautrec, who was only born in 1864, and thus probably wouldn't have therefore dreamed it up and introduced it to the larger society at the tender age of three.

In any case, the classic Earthquake combines two very French alcohols, cognac and absinthe, and can be sweetened or not, as the drinker desires. It seems rather scandalous that at the very least, this seemingly most French of mixed drinks was not on offer to Twain and his companions!

The Twentieth & Twenty-First Centuries

The twentieth century is truly the century of the cocktail, when a bewildering variety of mixed drinks showed up and inventive mixologists created new and delicious concoctions. The literary world reflected this new reality, as well, with these innovative serves becoming associated with many fictional characters, as well as their authors. Here is a generous pour of some of the best examples from some of the great works of modern literature.

Whiskey & Soda

"The Aunt and the Sluggard", P. G. Wodehouse, 1916

2 parts whiskey *1 part club soda*

Fill a Collins glass with ice.

Add the ingredients, gently stir until chilled, and enjoy.

I had a bit of dinner somewhere and went to a show of some kind; but nothing seemed to make any difference. I simply hadn't the heart to go on to supper anywhere. I just sucked down a whisky-and-soda in the hotel smoking-room and went straight up to bed. I don't know when I've felt so rotten.

Poor Bertie Wooster is left without the services of his trusty valet, Jeeves, for a brief time and can barely function (Jeeves is busy attending to one of Bertie's friends). And so, he consoles himself with a Whiskey & Soda and goes to bed.

A Whiskey & Soda might be the magic bullet for a sulking upper-class twit, but it can be enjoyed by anyone. This simple cocktail, made with any whiskey you like and a good dash of soda, is as simple and satisfying as can be.

Brandy & Soda

The Inimitable Jeeves, P. G. Wodehouse, 1923

---

2 parts brandy *1 part club soda*

Fill a Collins glass with ice.

Add the ingredients, gently stir until chilled, and enjoy.

"I say, Jeeves," I said.

"Sir?"

"Mix me a stiffish brandy and soda."

"Yes, sir."

"Stiffish, Jeeves. Not too much soda, but splash the brandy about a bit."

"Very good, sir."

After imbibing, I felt a shade better.

Bertie always finds that a good, stiff drink eases the discomfort of whatever absurd situation he's gotten himself into, and thankfully, Jeeves is (usually) on hand to handle everything else. Like the Whiskey & Soda, this concoction is very simple, and you can choose how much of each portion you wish to put in your drink. Bertie clearly prefers a more generous dash of brandy, but that's up to you.

Green Swizzle

"The Rummy Affair of Old Biffy", P. G. Wodehouse, 1924

---

1 part white rum

1 part absinthe

Dash of crème de menthe

1 sprig of fresh mint, for garnish

Place the rum and absinthe in a cocktail shaker, fill it two-thirds of the way with ice, and shake until chilled.

Strain over ice into a rocks glass and top with the crème de menthe.

Garnish with the sprig of mint and enjoy.

The man behind the counter, as kindly a bloke as I ever wish to meet, seemed to guess our requirements the moment we hove in view. Scarcely had our elbows touched the wood before he was leaping to and fro, bringing down a new bottle with each leap. A planter, apparently, does not consider he has had a drink unless it contains at least seven ingredients, and I'm not saying, mind you, that he isn't right. The man behind the bar told us the things were called Green Swizzles; and, if ever I marry and have a son, Green Swizzle Wooster is the name that will go down on the register, in memory of the day his father's life was saved at Wembley.

Bertie and his friend Biffy are bored at the British Empire Exhibition, and sneak off to a bar, where they encounter a wonderous new drink, the Green Swizzle. This heady elixir, a blend of rum, absinthe, and—usually—crème de menthe, must surely pack a punch, enough to save Bertie from dying of boredom, or so he claims.

Mint Julep

The Great Gatsby, F. Scott Fitzgerald, 1925

10 fresh mint leaves

1 teaspoon caster (superfine) sugar

Splash of water

2 oz. bourbon

1 sprig of fresh mint, for garnish

Place the mint leaves, sugar, and water in a Julep cup or highball glass and muddle.

Fill the glass with crushed ice, add the bourbon, and stir until chilled. Garnish with the sprig of mint and enjoy.

The notion originated with Daisy's suggestion that we hire five bathrooms and take cold baths, and then assumed more tangible form as "a place to have a mint julep." Each of us said over and over that it was a "crazy idea"—we all talked at once to a baffled clerk and thought, or pretended to think, that we were being very funny...

As Gatsby and his friends try to beat the heat on a particularly sweltering summer day, they find themselves at the Plaza Hotel, where Daisy suggests cold water immersion and Mint Juleps. The Mint Juleps seem a good idea, though the conversation becomes as heated as the weather before they can be enjoyed.

A classic hot weather cocktail, the Mint Julep is the traditional drink of the Kentucky Derby, a refreshing blend of bourbon, mint, sugar, and crushed ice that's sure to take the heat out of any situation. Well, almost any.

Gin Rickey

The Great Gatsby, F. Scott Fitzgerald, 1925

2 parts gin

1 part fresh lime juice

4 parts club soda

1 lime wedge, for garnish

Place the gin and lime juice in a cocktail shaker, fill it two-thirds of the way with ice, and shake until chilled.

Strain over ice into a highball glass, top with the club soda, and gently stir.

Garnish with the lime wedge and enjoy.

Tom came back, preceding four gin rickeys that clicked full of ice.

Gatsby took up his drink.

"They certainly look cool," he said, with visible tension.

We drank in long, greedy swallows.

Once again mindful of the heat, this time back at Gatsby's mansion, the friends indulge in the Gin Rickey, an easy-to-make drink that combines gin, lime, and soda. It's said to have been named for a Washington D.C. lobbyist, Joe Rickey, who preferred drinks that weren't sweet. His version was originally bourbon, but a gin variant soon appeared and became all the rage—enough so that it found its way into Fitzgerald's immortal tale, and was said to be one of the author's favorite drinks.

Bronx Cocktail

The Great Gatsby, F. Scott Fitzgerald, 1925

1½ oz. London dry gin

½ oz. sweet vermouth

½ oz. dry vermouth

1 oz. fresh orange juice

Chill a cocktail glass in the freezer.

Place all of the ingredients in a cocktail shaker, fill it two-thirds of the way with ice, and shake until chilled.

Double-strain into the chilled glass and enjoy.

Every Friday five crates of oranges and lemons arrived from a fruiterer in New York—every Monday these same oranges and lemons left his back door in a pyramid of pulpless halves. There was a machine in the kitchen which could extract the juice of two hundred oranges in half an hour if a little button was pressed two hundred times by a butler's thumb.

The Bronx Cocktail is not specifically mentioned in *The Great Gatsby*, but in 1914, a young Fitzgerald had sent a telegram to his new girlfriend, extolling the wonders of the drink, claiming that he and his friend drank several in a row. Given that freshly squeezed orange juice is a key ingredient in this cocktail, it's entirely possible that this was the drink that Fitzgerald had in mind when he wrote that Gatsby was having large amount of citrus delivered.

Most often a blend of gin and sweet and dry vermouth with orange juice, legend says that the drink was created in the early 1900s and named for the Bronx Zoo. But wherever it came from, it's sure to be enjoyable, even without Gatsby's lavish parties and productions as a backdrop.

Jack Rose

The Sun Also Rises, Ernest Hemmingway, 1926

1 oz. applejack

½ oz. grenadine

Seltzer, to top

Place the applejack and grenadine in a mixing glass, fill it two-thirds of the way with ice, and stir until chilled.

Strain into a coupe, top with seltzer, and enjoy.

At five o'clock I was in the Hotel Crillon waiting for Brett. She was not there, so I sat down and wrote some letters. They were not very good letters but I hoped their being on Crillon stationery would help them. Brett did not turn up, so about quarter to six I went down to the bar and had a Jack Rose with George the barman.

In a Paris hotel, narrator Jake Barnes waits for Lady Brett Ashley, the woman he's drawn to but with whom he is doomed never to have a real relationship. When she fails to turn up, he passes the time by drinking a Jack Rose in the bar. There are many different origin stories for the Jack Rose, but it seems to have first shown up in the early twentieth century. Its name probably simply refers to its main ingredients, applejack (apple brandy) and grenadine, which gives it a rose-colored hue. The Jack Rose can be enjoyed by anyone, doomed lovers or not!

Hangman's Blood

A High Wind in Jamaica, Richard Hughes, 1929

1 part rum

1 part gin

1 part brandy

1 part porter

Fill a Collins glass with ice.

Add all of the ingredients, stir until chilled, and enjoy.

Captain Jonsen ... went on board, and mixed several gallons of that potion known in alcoholic circles as Hangman's Blood (which is compounded of rum, gin, brandy, and porter). Innocent (merely beery) as it looks, refreshing as its tastes, it has the property of increasing rather than allaying thirst, and so, once it has made a breach, soon demolishes the whole fort.

In this tale, Jonsen is a pirate who has kidnapped several children and young people on their way home from Jamaica, which is far darker and stranger than the usual "abducted by pirates" fare. Jonsen here is trying to get in good with a group of Cubans at a Havana dock and uses a very strong drink to win them over. As you can see from the description, it packs quite the punch! It seems that Hughes invented this drink, and even if he meant it more as a joke, many have since tried making it and enjoyed it. So have a swashbuckling adventure, if you dare!

Satan's Whisker

Black Coffee,
Agatha Christie, 1930, adapted by Charles Osborne

1 part brandy

1 part crème de menthe

Dash of cayenne pepper

Place the ingredients in a mixing glass, fill it two-thirds of the way with ice, and stir until chilled.

Strain the cocktail into a double rocks glass and enjoy.

"Now what would really pull Lucia around in no time would be a Satan's Whisker."

Miss Amory turned a shocked countenance upon her niece. "What," she enquired in horrified tones, "might a Satan's Whisker be?"

"It's quite simple to make, if you have the ingredients," replied Barbara. "It's merely equal parts of brandy and crème de menthe, but you mustn't forget a shake of red pepper. That's most important. It's absolutely super, and guaranteed to put some pep into you."

A Poirot mystery involving a stolen secret nuclear formula and the murder of the man who invented it, this play was later turned into a novel. It has all the classic elements of a Christie murder mystery, including the need for some of the suspects to calm their nerves, or in this case, invigorate themselves a bit. There are a number of versions of the Satan's Whisker, including those made of vermouth and brandy, but Christie's recipe here seems to work quite well. The dash of hot chile pepper will definitely put some pep into the drinker!

Manhattan

The Glass Key, Dashiell Hammett, 1931

2 oz. rye whiskey

⅔ oz. sweet vermouth

2 drops of aromatic bitters

1 maraschino cherry, for garnish

Chill a cocktail glass in the freezer. Place the rye, vermouth, and bitters in a mixing glass, fill it two-thirds of the way with ice, and stir until chilled.

Strain into the chilled glass, garnish with the maraschino cherry, and enjoy.

The bar-tender, a fat man with a spongy nose, said: "Evening, Ned. We ain't been seeing you much lately."

"Lo, Jimmy. Been behaving. Manhattan."

The bar-tender began to mix the cocktail. The orchestra finished its piece. A woman's voice rose thin and shrill: "I won't stay in the same place with that Beaumont bastard."

The Glass Key is a classic detective story from the man who created Sam Spade and *The Maltese Falcon*. In this story, the protagonist is one Ned Beaumont, an amateur detective whose connections to organized crime hardly make him a sterling example of a hero. In this case, he's investigating the murder of a senator's son that seems to have far more sinister implications.

But of course, being a tough-as-nails detective, he has to drink regularly. In this scene, his drink of choice is the old reliable Manhattan, a blend of rye whiskey, sweet vermouth, and bitters. One story says that it was originally created for Lady Randolph Churchill (Winston Churchill's mother), when she threw a lavish party at New York's legendary Manhattan Club in 1874.

Bourbon & Coke

The Postman Always Rings Twice, James M. Cain, 1934

2 parts bourbon

1 part Coca-Cola

1 lemon twist, for garnish

Fill a mason jar with ice.

Add the bourbon and soda and stir until chilled.

Garnish with the lemon twist and enjoy.

I went to my room and got the liquor. It was a quart of Bourbon, three quarters full. I went down, got some Coca Cola glasses, and ice cubes, and White Rock, and came back upstairs. She had taken her hat off and let her hair down. I fixed two drinks. They had some White Rock in them, and a couple of pieces of ice, but the rest was out of the bottle.

Technically, this recipe calls for bourbon and White Rock soda, but since the glasses were Coke glasses, the substitution of Coca-Cola is entirely appropriate. This controversial novel follows the exploits of Frank and Cora, two lovers who plot to murder Cora's older husband. Unfortunately for them, everything keeps going wrong, and it all turns out very badly for both of them. Their only relief might have been to drink more Bourbon and Coke!

It's a simple recipe with just the two named ingredients and perhaps a lemon twist to give it a bit more zing. Murder plots not required. Or recommended.

Knickerbocker Martini

The Thin Man, Dashiell Hammett, 1934

3 parts gin

1 part dry vermouth

1 part sweet vermouth

2 to 3 dashes of aromatic bitters

1 lemon twist, for garnish

Place the gin, vermouths, and bitters in a mixing glass, fill it two-thirds of the way with ice, and stir until chilled.

Strain into a cocktail glass, garnish with the lemon twist, and enjoy.

"How about shaking up a drink?"

She mixed some cocktails. I was on my second or third when she came back from answering the telephone and said: "Your friend Mimi wants to talk to you."

Hammet's *Thin Man* tells the tale of private detective Nick, and his wife Nora, during the days of Prohibition, when few took such laws seriously. The book refers to them constantly pouring cocktails for themselves and others, while also trying to solve the mystery of the murder of an old client's secretary. The book is short on specifics for which drinks are involved, while the film adaptation from the same year goes into much more detail about their preferred beverages. The always-tipsy couple enjoy their Martinis, among other drinks, so this seems a perfect moment to celebrate the classic cocktail.

According to one legend, the Martini was invented at the Knickerbocker Hotel in New York, by a bartender named Martini di Arma di Taggia. When he served one to John D. Rockefeller in 1906, Rockefeller was so enamored of the drink that he insisted on naming it after the bartender.

Pink Gin

Three Act Tragedy, Agatha Christie, 1934

1½ oz. gin

2 to 3 dashes of Angostura Bitters

1 strip of lemon peel

Pinch of lemon zest, for garnish

Place the gin and bitters in a rocks glass filled with ice and stir until chilled.

Express the strip of lemon peel over the cocktail and then discard the lemon peel.

Garnish with the lemon zest and enjoy.

"Upsettin' sort of time, wasn't it?" he said. "Up in Yorkshire, I mean. Something rather amusin' about a doctor being poisoned—you see what I mean—wrong way about. A doctor's a chap who poisons other people."

He laughed uproariously at his own remark and ordered another pink gin.

Another Poirot mystery, this time involving the mysterious death of a clergyman, Reverend Babbington, after drinking some port. And yet, there are no traces of poison in the glass. A second death, that of Sir Charles Strange, only adds to the mystery. Captain Dacres considers the whole thing rather amusing, as this little scene shows, and orders another Pink Gin.

The Pink Gin seems to have originated in the British Navy in the 1820s, and is simplicity itself, being simply a blend of gin with a dash of dark red Angostura Bitters, which give the drink its pink color. More modern versions sometimes use ice, soda, and citrus slices as garnishes, but the original recipe is perfectly fine on its own, especially when foul play is afoot.

Sidecar

Trinity Town, Norman Collins, 1936

Sugar, for the rim (optional)

1½ oz. cognac

¾ oz. Cointreau

¾ oz. fresh lemon juice

1 lemon twist, for garnish

If desired, wet the rim of a coupe and coat it with sugar.

Place the cognac, Cointreau, and lemon juice in a cocktail shaker, fill it two-thirds of the way with ice, and shake until chilled.

Strain into the coupe, garnish with the lemon twist, and enjoy.

"What would you like—a Bronx or a Sidecar?"

"A Sidecar," Vicky told him. She had never had a cocktail before.

Collins wrote a number of novels about contemporary British life, but he was more famous for his work with the BBC, first in radio and then in television. He resigned from the BBC in 1950 over creative conflicts, but he continued to work to make television a household necessity in Britain from the 1950s onward, and he championed new programming and broadcasting corporations, remaining active up until just before he died in 1982.

The Sidecar was probably invented during or just after World War I and usually consists of cognac blended with Cointreau or another orange liqueur, and lemon juice. As a choice for one's first cocktail, it might be a bit strong, but still not a bad option!

Hock & Seltzer

"The Arrest of Oscar Wilde at the Cadogan Hotel", John Betjeman, 1937

---

2 parts Riesling

2 parts soda water

1 orange slice, for garnish

Fill a cocktail glass with ice and add the Riesling.

Top with the soda water and gently stir.

Garnish with the orange slice and enjoy.

He sipped at a weak hock and seltzer

As he gazed at the London skies

Through the Nottingham lace of the curtains

Or was it his bees-winged eyes?

Betjeman's poem imagines the moments before Oscar Wilde was arrested in April 1895, and later charged with gross indecency. Wilde was known to be fond of absinthe and Champagne, but here, Betjeman has him casually sipping on Hock and Seltzer.

"Hock" is a British term for German white wine, often from the Rhein region, and often Riesling. So, this drink is simply a blend of this kind of wine with soda water to give it some sparkle. It was a popular drink in nineteenth-century Britain, so Wilde certainly would have known of it, and probably been fond of it. Here he also knows what fate awaits him, but he's going out in style, as usual!

Champagne Cocktail

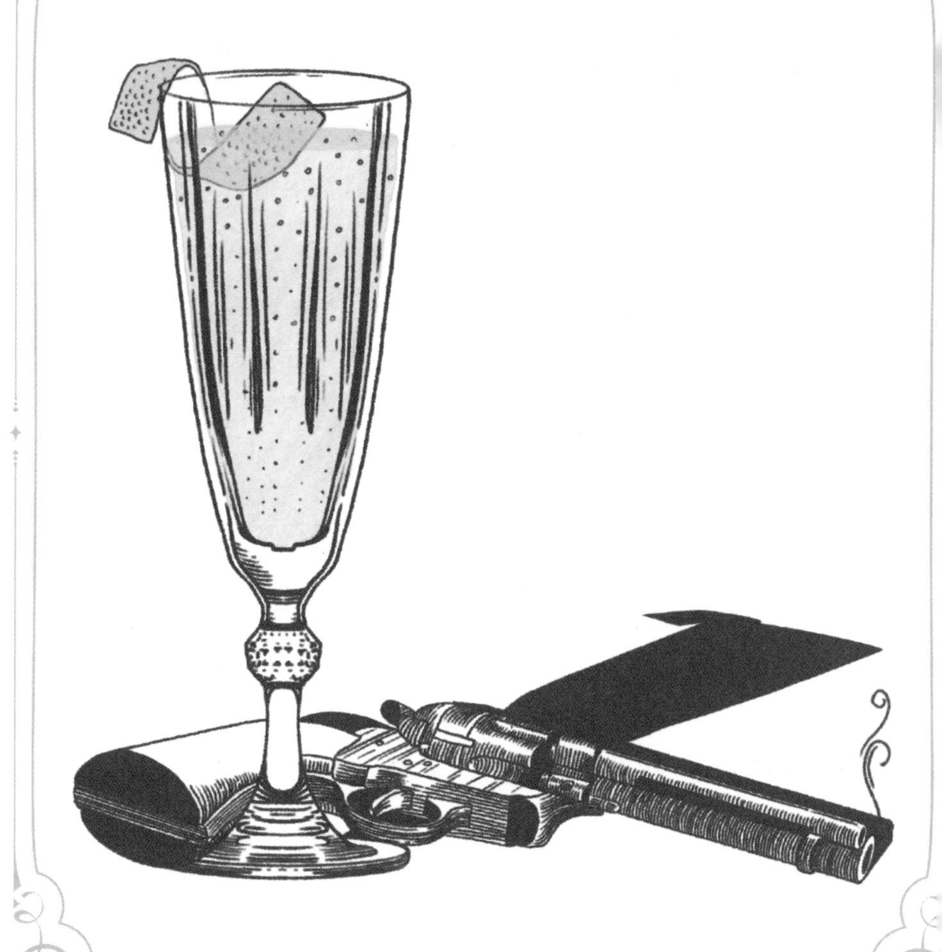

The Big Sleep, Raymond Chandler, 1939

1 part brandy
2 parts Champagne
1 lemon twist, for garnish

Fill a cocktail glass with ice and add the brandy.

Top with the Champagne, garnish with the lemon twist, and enjoy.

"When the General is feeling a little better—possibly tomorrow—he would like to thank you in person."

"Fine," I said. "I'll come out and drink some more of his brandy, maybe with champagne."

"I shall see that some is properly iced," the old boy said, almost with a smirk in his voice. That was that.

This novel is a classic Philip Marlowe detective story, wherein Marlowe tries to help one General Sternwood solve a blackmail case. All gets resolved, but it isn't long before murder is on the menu, too. Marlowe is a hard-drinking private eye, but he's not averse to the finer things in life, and here, he wants to sample some of the general's finest alcohols, in this case his brandy and his Champagne in a cocktail. He's assured that the drink will be waiting for him.

A different mixture than Twain's Champagne Cock-Tail (see page 44), this blend of Champagne and brandy might be just the thing to intensify those lingering doubts about a crime, but it might also just be an indulgence for a fine evening, no blackmail required.

May Queen

Uncle Fred in the Springtime, P. G. Wodehouse, 1939

1 oz. brandy

1 oz. kummel

½ oz. Armagnac

½ oz. Yellow Chartreuse

Stout, to taste

1 oz. Champagne

Chill a cocktail glass in the freezer.

Place all of the ingredients, except for the Champagne, in a cocktail shaker, fill it two-thirds of the way with ice, and shake vigorously until chilled.

Strain into the chilled cocktail glass, top with the Champagne, and enjoy.

Do we by any chance know a beverage called May Queen? Its full name is "To-morrow'll be of all the year the maddest, merriest day, for I'm to be Queen of the May, mother, I'm to be Queen of the May." A clumsy title, generally shortened for purposes of ordinary conversation. Its foundation is any good, dry champagne, to which is added liqueur brandy, Armagnac, kummel, yellow chartreuse and old stout, to taste. It is a good many years since I tried it myself, but I can thoroughly recommend it to alleviate the deepest despondency.

Uncle Fred is yet another whimsical tale by Wodehouse, though this one involves not Jeeves and Wooster, but the author's other memorable (if clueless) creation, Clarence, Earl of Emsworth and his magnificent home, Blandings Castle. The story follows any number of amusing schemes and plots, including the plan to abduct the earl's prized pig.

As such, a good stiff drink might well be called for, and the May Queen sounds like a heady mix to be sure!

Absinthe Shaken

For Whom the Bell Tolls, Ernest Hemingway, 1940

1½ oz. absinthe

½ oz. simple syrup

2 oz. water

1 sprig of fresh mint, for garnish

Place the absinthe, syrup, and water in a cocktail shaker, fill it two-thirds of the way with ice, and shake until chilled.

Fill a cocktail glass with crushed ice and strain the cocktail over it. Garnish with the sprig of mint and enjoy.

"It smells of anis but it is bitter as gall," he said. "It is better to be sick than have that medicine."

"That's the wormwood," Robert Jordan told him. "In this, the real absinthe, there is wormwood. It's supposed to rot your brain out but I don't believe it. It only changes the ideas. You should pour water into it very slowly, a few drops at a time."

Hemingway's classic is set during the Spanish Civil War, an event he knew only too well, given that he was in Spain, on the ground, reporting on events. The story follows the tragic tale of American Robert Jordan, who fights against the Fascists. His specialty is blowing up bridges, but his days are numbered.

In the scene above, Jordan is offering absinthe up as a medicine, and claiming that it can cure anything that ails someone. Absinthe was, of course, a seemingly dangerous and forbidden drink for decades (it was banned in the United States until 2007), over fears that it could drive drinkers mad (which is not true, happy to say!). As for being medicinal? Well, in a pinch, it probably couldn't hurt.

Alexandra

Brideshead Revisited, Evelyn Waugh, 1945

1 oz. gin or rum

2 oz. crème de cacao

2 oz. coffee liqueur

4 oz. crème fraîche

Place all of the ingredients in cocktail shaker, fill it two-thirds of the way with ice, and shake until chilled.

Strain into a cocktail glass and enjoy.

At the George bar he ordered "Four Alexandra cocktails, please," ranged them before him with a loud "Yum-yum" which drew every eye, outraged, upon him. "I expect you would prefer sherry, but, my dear Charles, you are not going to have sherry. Isn't this a delicious concoction? You don't like it? Then I will drink it for you."

Protagonist Charles Ryder, while studying at Oxford, finds himself periodically in the company of self-proclaimed aesthete Anthony Blanche. On this occasion, Blanche makes a bit of a spectacle of himself while threatening to down all of the alcohol set before him.

The drink in question is the Alexandra, related to the Alexander Cocktail and the Brandy Alexander. Usually consisting of cream, gin or rum, crème de cacao, and coffee liqueur, it is quite decadent and rich. Knocking back four of them would be quite the feat, and probably inadvisable!

Beer Milkshake

Cannery Row, John Steinbeck, 1945

4 scoops of vanilla ice cream
2 oz. stout
2 oz. chocolate fudge
Chocolate syrup, to drizzle
Dollop of whipped cream, for garnish

Place the ice cream, stout, and chocolate fudge in a blender and puree until smooth.

Line the inside of a frozen glass with drizzles of chocolate syrup and pour the milkshake into the glass.

Garnish with the whipped cream and enjoy.

Blaisedell, the poet, had said to him: "You love beer so much. I'll bet some day you'll go in and order a beer milkshake." It was a simple piece of foolery, but it had bothered Doc ever since. He wondered what a beer milk-shake would taste like. The idea gagged him, but he couldn't let it alone. It cropped up every time he had a glass of beer. Would it curdle the milk? Would you add sugar? It was like a shrimp ice-cream. Once the thing got into your head you couldn't forget it.

Cannery Row follows a group of people whose lives intertwine on a street of the same name, in Monterey, California, during the Great Depression. Doc is a marine biologist, and when several people want to throw a party for him, things get out of hand, carrying far beyond the playful idea of mixing milk and beer.

While it doesn't sound too appetizing, the Beer Milkshake has its devotees, and recent recipes have tended to use a quality stout beer and add ice cream to make it more of a proper milkshake, just with beer added in. Think of a root beer float, all grown up.

Very Dry Martini

Catcher in the Rye, J. D. Salinger, 1951

3 oz. London dry gin

½ oz. dry vermouth

1 lemon twist, for garnish

Chill a cocktail glass in the freezer.

Place the gin and vermouth in a mixing glass, fill it two-thirds of the way with ice, and stir until chilled.

Strain into the chilled glass, garnish with the lemon twist, and enjoy.

I didn't say anything for a while. I let it drop for a while. Then old Luce ordered another Martini and told the bartender to make it a lot dryer.

This novel was originally intended for adults, but has become a classic for generations of younger readers due to its critique of the hypocritical adult world. The main character, Holden Caulfield, finds himself at odds with his world at almost every turn. In this scene, he is talking with an old schoolmate, Carl Luce, at the Wicker Bar in New York, and trying to tease out of him all manner of things relating to sex and Luce's sexuality. Luce orders the driest Martini possible.

"Dry" in this case refers to favoring a heavier alcoholic content, so that there would be far more gin than vermouth in a Dry Martini (as much as seven times more in some recipes!). The taste of the alcohol will be much stronger, perfect for navigating difficult conversations with old friends. Or not.

Scotch & Soda

1944 AUTO DRIVERS LICENSE
Issued to CAULFIELD
SIGNATURE OF LICENSE
Caulfield

Catcher in the Rye, J. D. Salinger, 1951

2 parts Scotch whisky | *1 part club soda*

Fill a mason jar or a rocks glass with ice.

Add the Scotch and club soda, gently stir, and enjoy.

I ordered a Scotch and soda, and told him not to mix it—I said it fast as hell, because if you hem and haw, they think you're under twenty-one and won't sell you any intoxicating liquor. I had trouble with him anyway, though.

"I'm sorry, sir," he said, "but do you have some verification of your age? Your driver's license, perhaps?"

I gave him this very cold stare, like he'd insulted the hell out of me, and asked him, "Do I look like I'm under twenty-one?"

Caulfield attempts to bluff his way at the bar, but the skeptical bartender doesn't give in, and Caulfield has to settle for a Coca-Cola. In this variant of the classic Scotch & Soda, you can try not mixing the two ingredients overly, as our protagonist requests, and consider substituting rye whiskey to better honor the book's title.

Vesper Martini

Casino Royale, Ian Fleming, 1953

6 parts gin

2 parts vodka

1 part Lillet Blanc

1 strip of lemon peel, for garnish

Place the gin, vodka, and Lillet in a cocktail shaker, fill it two-thirds of the way with ice, and shake until chilled.

Strain into a cocktail glass, garnish with the strip of lemon peel, and enjoy.

"A dry Martini," he said. "One. In a deep champagne goblet."

"Oui, Monsieur."

"Just a moment. Three measures of Gordon's, one of vodka, half a measure of Kina Lillet. Shake it very well until it's ice-cold, then add a large thin slice of lemon peel. Got it?"

"Certainly, monsieur." The barman seemed pleased with the idea.

James Bond, his suaveness never in doubt, makes a special order for the "Vesper" Martini, named after double agent Vesper Lynd, an obligatory Bond love interest. Gordon's is a classic British gin, and while Kina Lillet is no longer produced, Lillet Blanc, a French aperitif that blends wine, fruits, liqueur, and spices, is an able substitute. The two added to a bit of vodka will make for something special, even though none of us will ever look as cool as Bond when drinking it.

Gimlet

The Long Good-Bye, Raymond Chandler, 1953

1½ oz. gin

½ oz. fresh lime juice

1 lime twist, for garnish

Place the gin and lime juice in a cocktail shaker, fill it two-thirds of the way with ice, and shake until chilled.

Strain into a cocktail glass, garnish with the lime twist, and enjoy.

We sat in a corner of the bar at Victor's and drank gimlets.

"They don't know how to make them here," he said. "What they call a gimlet is just some lime or lemon juice and gin with a dash of sugar and bitters. A real gimlet is half gin and half Rose's Lime Juice and nothing else. It beats martinis hollow."

Another novel featuring Chandler's beloved private eye, Philip Marlowe. Marlowe befriends a man named Terry Lennox and the two enjoy spending time in a Los Angeles nightclub, drinking Gimlets. Later, Lennox flees to Mexico and his wife turns up dead, and that's just the beginning of Marlowe's troubles!

Before the adventure begins, the two enjoy drinking and bantering, and Lennox insists that their local can't make a proper Gimlet, which is simpler than what they're drinking. Indeed, modern recipes for the Gimlet often add simple syrup into the mix, but you might want to try Lennox's version, if you can.

The Gimlet seems to have been introduced in the British Navy in the later eighteenth century and was useful for preventing scurvy among sailors. At least, that was the excuse of those who imbibed.

Webster F. Street Lay-Away Plan

Sweet Thursday, John Steinbeck, 1954

4 parts Tanqueray gin

1 part Green Chartreuse

1 lemon twist, for garnish

Place the gin and Chartreuse in a mixing glass, fill it two-thirds of the way with ice, and stir until chilled.

Strain into a cocktail glass, garnish with the lemon twist, and enjoy.

"How's about a cocktail? The wine's cooling."

Doc said, "One time I had some kind of—"

"I remember!" said Sonny Boy. "The Webster F. Street Lay-Away Plan—a martini made with chartreuse instead of vermouth. Very good."

"Very effective, as I remember it," said Doc.

In this sequel to *Cannery Row*, the main character, Doc, returns to Monterey, California, after serving in World War II. He discovers that things have changed and he struggles to reopen his old business. Various characters try to set him up with newcomer Suzy, and in this scene, they are in a restaurant and bar, where the proprietor, Sonny Boy, recommends a unique version of a Martini.

As Sonny Boy says, this Martini is made with Chartreuse, a French herbal liqueur which undoubtedly gives it a unique flavor, quite different from the traditional drink. Give it a try if you're in the mood for something new, or maybe trying to impress your date.

Pin

Lolita, Vladimir Nabokov, 1955

1 part gin

1 part pineapple juice

1 part soda water

2 dashes of simple syrup

1 pineapple slice, for garnish

Fill a mason jar with ice.

Add all of the ingredients and stir until chilled.

Garnish with the pineapple slice and enjoy.

The sun made its usual round of the house as the afternoon ripened into evening. I had a drink. And another. And yet another. Gin and pineapple juice, my favourite mixture, always doubled my energy.

Lolita has been a controversial book since it was first published, and became even more so after Stanley Kubrick made a film adaptation in 1962. The story of a middle-aged professor who becomes infatuated with a twelve-year-old girl was and remains too much for many critics and readers, though the book was meant as a critique, not an endorsement. The author even referred to the novel's depraved narrator, Humbert Humbert, as "a vain and cruel wretch."

The word "Pin" is the narrator's portmanteau of "pineapple and gin" and is his favorite drink. It's a refreshing concoction, sometimes made with the addition of simple syrup and soda water. And don't worry, it can be enjoyed on its own, without any concerns about its affiliation with one of modern literature's most unsavory characters.

Wine Spodiodi

On the Road, Jack Kerouac, 1957

2 parts port *1 part whiskey*

Place the port and whiskey in a cocktail shaker, fill it two-thirds of the way with ice, and shake until chilled.

Strain into a cocktail glass and enjoy.

Dean and I had ended up with a colored guy called Walter who ordered drinks at the bar and had them lined up and said, "Wine-spodiodi!" which was a shot of port wine, a shot of whisky, and a shot of port wine. "Nice sweet jacket for all that bad whisky!" he yelled.

Kerouac's classic about the travels of Sal Paradise and Dean Moriarty through the United States from 1947 to 1950 is filled with jazz, booze, and the Beat scene. It's an autobiography of sorts for the author, who made his own similar trips during those years. In this scene, the two characters are in San Francisco, and getting ready to drive back east, when they meet an enthusiastic man at a bar who orders a drink that's unfamiliar to them, the Wine Spodiodi.

This blend of two parts port and one part whiskey will pack a punch, but is delicious, even if you're not off on an epic road trip. And there's no need to use a bad whiskey when a good one will make it taste that much better!

Daiquiri

Our Man in Havana, Graham Greene, 1958

2 oz. lightly aged rum

½ oz. fresh lime juice

1 teaspoon caster (superfine) sugar

1 lime wheel, for garnish

Chill a coupe in the freezer.

Place the rum, lime juice, and sugar in a cocktail shaker, fill it two-thirds of the way with ice, and shake until chilled.

Strain into the chilled coupe, garnish with the lime wheel, and enjoy.

"Have you ever seen so many whiskies?"

"As a matter of fact I have. I collect miniatures and I have ninety-nine at home."

"Interesting. And what's your choice today? A dimpled Haig?"

"Thanks, I've just ordered a daiquiri."

"Can't take those things. They relax me."

This satirical novel, set in Cuba before the rise of Fidel Castro, mocks intelligence services. In Cuba, a vacuum salesman, James Wormold, is approached about doing work for British intelligence. He agrees, but having nothing to report, he starts making things up. In this scene, Wormold is sounded out about his drink preferences, and he goes with a Daiquiri, a Caribbean-themed cocktail that is not the adult frozen slushie you might think of when you hear the word—the original version of the drink (that was probably invented in the late nineteenth century) is simply rum mixed with sugar and lime.

White Angel

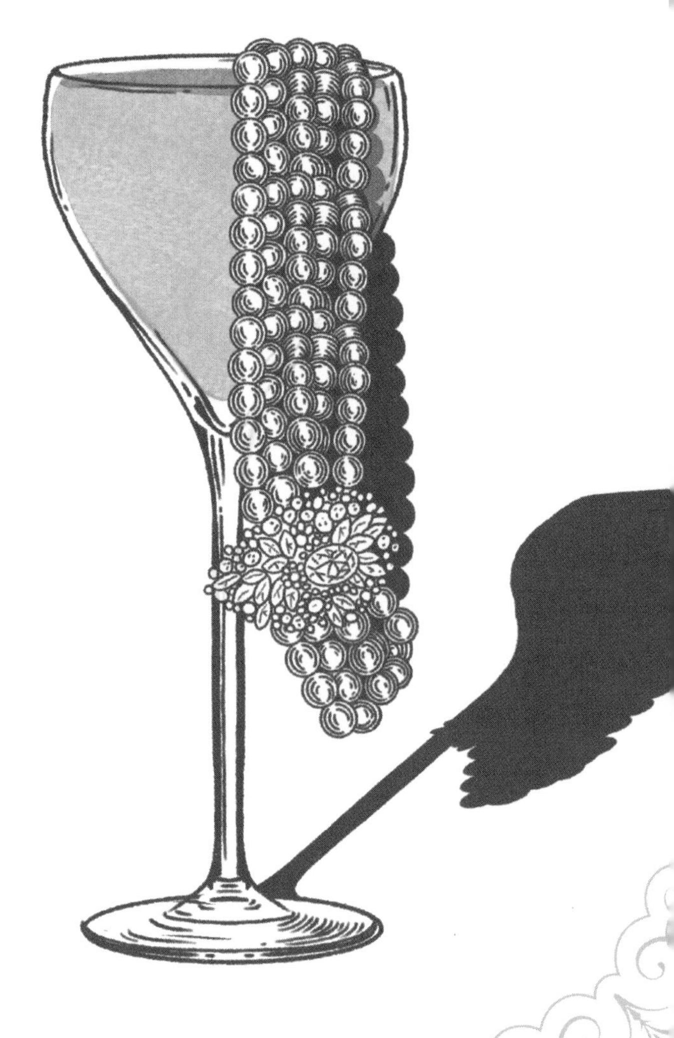

Breakfast at Tiffany's, Truman Capote, 1958

1 part vodka | *1 part gin*

Place vodka and gin in a cocktail shaker, fill it two-thirds of the way with ice, and shake until chilled.

Strain into a cocktail glass and enjoy.

"Let me build you a drink. Something new. They call it a White Angel," he said, mixing one-half vodka, one-half gin, no vermouth. While I drank the result, Joe Bell stood sucking on a Tums and turning over in his mind what he had to tell me.

Capote's novella is undoubtedly more famous because of the (loose) film adaptation starring Audrey Hepburn from 1961. The film is more light-hearted than the book, which definitely takes a darker turn. Set in the 1940s and 1950s, a narrator (who is never named) befriends a mysterious young woman named Holly Golightly, who has a shadowy past. This scene takes place right at the beginning of the novel, when the narrator is hoping to hear some news about Holly, who he's not seen for some time.

While he waits, he tries "something new," a simple cocktail that will undoubtedly pack a bit of a punch. You can experiment with different types of both gin and vodka, or stick with the classics, especially if you're searching for a long-lost someone.

Gibson

Playback, Raymond Chandler, 1958

4 parts gin

1 part dry vermouth

Pickled onion, for garnish

Place the gin and vermouth in a mixing glass, fill the glass two-thirds of the way with ice, and stir until chilled.

Strain into a cocktail glass, garnish with the pickled onion, and enjoy.

The dining room was dim, candlelit, divided by a low wall into two halves. It would have looked crowded with thirty people in it. The captain shoved me in a corner and lit my candle for me. I said I would have a double Gibson. A waiter came up and started to remove the place setting on the far side of the table. I told him to leave it, a friend might join me...

The Gibson arrived. I could make out the shape of the glass and there seemed to be something in it. I tasted it and it wasn't too bad.

Another Philip Marlowe adventure, this time the private eye is on the trail of a woman named Betty Mayfield, a woman fleeing from a troubled past. They both end up in a small town just north of San Diego, and, as always, things go from bad to worse. In this scene, Marlowe encounters another investigator and they have a heated exchange.

But at least Marlowe has his drink. The Gibson (in this case, a double) is simply a Martini, a blend of gin and vermouth, but instead of a twist or an olive, it's garnished with a pickled onion. It's a drink that seems to fit with Marlowe's tough exterior, and the flavor is intriguing enough that's well worth a try! PS, in the interest of keeping things on the level, this recipe is for a single.

Tom Collins

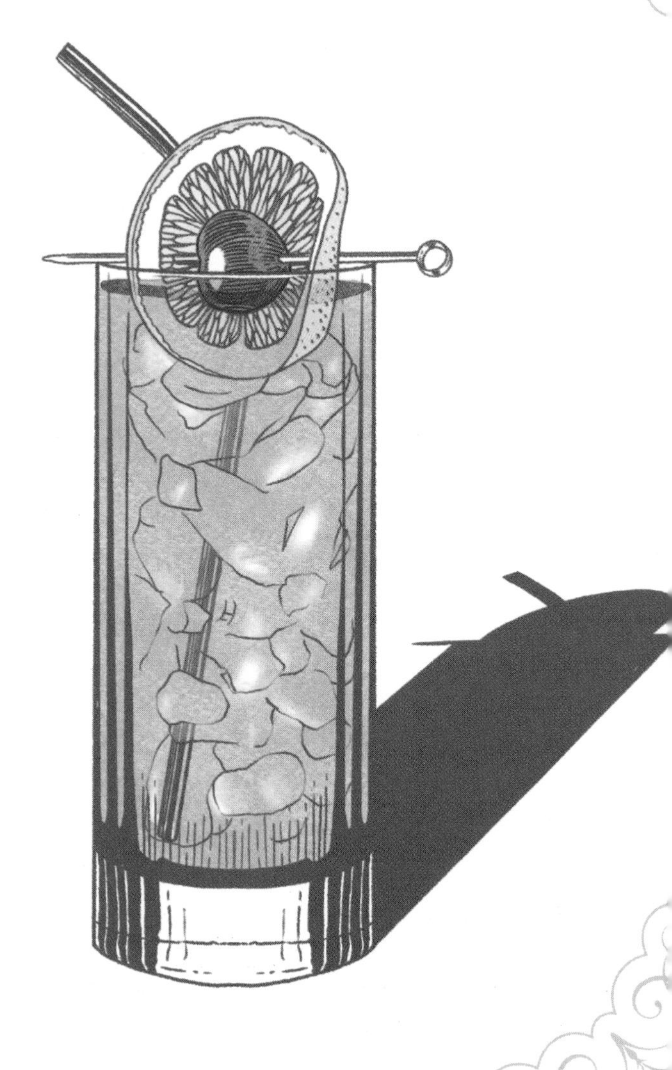

"The Small Rain", Thomas Pynchon, 1959

2 oz. Old Tom gin

1 oz. simple syrup

¾ oz. fresh lemon juice

Club soda, to top

1 lemon wheel, for garnish

1 maraschino cherry, for garnish

Fill a Collins glass with ice and chill it in the freezer.

Place the gin, syrup, and lemon juice in a cocktail shaker, fill it two-thirds of the way with ice, and shake until chilled.

Strain into the chilled Collins glass and top with the club soda. Garnish with the lemon wheel and cherry and enjoy.

"Hey," he said, "what y'all drinking?"

"Tom Collins," she said.

Levine drank scotch. Her face got serious.

"Is it bad out there?" she said.

"The Small Rain" is a short story from a larger collection of Pynchon stories, *Slow Learner*. The story takes place in 1957, during the aftermath of a hurricane in Louisiana. The main character, Nathan "Lardass" Levine, is an army private who's part of the cleanup operation. Normally a slacker, he begins to take the job seriously once he sees the gravity of the situation.

The Tom Collins is a cocktail from London dating to the later nineteenth century, and its name might have come from a bartender named John Collins, and the use of Old Tom gin. Or it might be something else entirely!

Old Fashioned

Rabbit, Run, John Updike, 1960

1 sugar cube

2 drops of bitters

Splash of water

2 oz. bourbon

1 orange slice, for garnish

1 maraschino cherry, for garnish

Place the sugar cube in a rocks glass and saturate it with the bitters. Add the water and muddle.

Fill the glass with ice and add the bourbon.

Gently stir, garnish with the slice of orange and maraschino cherry, and enjoy.

"I was tired."

"No wonder," he says. "How many of those have you had?" He gestures at the Old-fashioned glass. Sugar has stained the side she drank from.

Rabbit, Run is the first of Updike's novels about Harry "Rabbit" Angstrom. The former high school basketball star, only in his twenties, fears that his best years are already behind him as he is stuck in a loveless marriage and a dead-end job. In this scene, one of many tense moments between him and his wife, Janice, he notices her heavy drinking, which is all the worse because she is pregnant with their second child.

Regardless of the novel's dark themes, the Old Fashioned is a favorite in the cocktail world. Although it possibly dates to the early part of the nineteenth century, it got its name in the later part of that century, showing that people already thought of it as "old fashioned" by then!

Brandy Alexander

Who's Afraid of Virginia Woolf?, Edward Albee, 1962

1 oz. brandy

2 oz. crème de cacao

4 oz. crème fraîche

Dash of nutmeg, for garnish

Place all of the ingredients, except for the nutmeg, in cocktail shaker, fill it two-thirds of the way with ice, and shake until chilled.

Strain into a cocktail glass, garnish with the dash of nutmeg, and enjoy.

We'd go into a bar... you know, a bar... a whiskey, beer, and bourbon bar... and what she'd do would be, she'd screw up her face, think real hard, and come up with... brandy Alexanders, creme de cacao frappes, gimlets, flaming punch bowls... seven-layer liqueur things.

Albee's play explores the tensions between a middle-aged married couple, Martha and George. George teaches history at a local college, while Martha is the daughter of the college's president. The play involves them inviting over a younger couple, Nick and Honey, and as the acts unfold, the tensions and delusions between George and Martha become clear. In this scene, near the beginning, George talks about his wife's love of "lady-like little drinkies" before they got married, including the Brandy Alexander.

A Brandy Alexander is indeed a special drink, related to the Alexandra on page 92. It consists of brandy, crème de cacao, and cream, and is usually garnished with nutmeg. This would make a fine winter holiday drink, in an academic setting or otherwise.

Whiskey Sour

The Crying of Lot 49, Thomas Pynchon, 1966

2 parts whiskey

1 part fresh lemon juice

Splash of water

Pinch of caster (superfine) sugar

1 maraschino cherry, for garnish

Fill a rocks glass with ice, add all of the ingredients, except for the garnish, and stir until chilled.

Garnish with the maraschino cherry and enjoy.

...then through the sunned gathering of her marjoram and sweet basil from the herb garden, reading of book reviews in the latest Scientific American *into the layering of a lasagna, garlicking of a bread, tearing up of romaine leaves, eventually, oven on, into the mixing of the twilight's whiskey sours against the arrival of her husband, Wendell ("Mucho") Maas from work...*

This satirical, postmodern novella tells the story of a California woman, Oedipa Maas. After hearing of the death of a former lover named Pierce Inverarity, Oedipa becomes convinced that a secret society called Trystero, which began as a postal service in eighteenth-century Europe, is now doing possibly nefarious things behind the scenes. Before all of that, though, she simply wants to make dinner and enjoy a few drinks with her husband.

The Whiskey Sour isn't particularly "sour," as that's commonly the name given to mixed drinks with citrus. The addition of egg white is optional, and many bars now serve the Whiskey Sour without it, for health reasons. It's up to you if you want to go all in with the traditional recipe or not. Just watch out for those underhanded postal services.

Frozen Daiquiri

Islands in the Stream, Ernest Hemingway, 1970

2 oz. lightly aged rum

½ oz. fresh lime juice

1 teaspoon caster (superfine) sugar

1 lime wheel, for garnish

Chill a large coupe in the freezer.

Place the rum, lime juice, and sugar in a blender, add ½ cup ice, and puree until smooth.

Pour the cocktail into the chilled coupe, garnish with the lime wheel, and enjoy.

He had drunk double frozen daiquiris, the great ones that Constante made, that had no taste of alcohol and felt, as you drank them, the way downhill glacier skiing feels running through powder snow and, after the sixth and eighth, felt like downhill glacier skiing feels when you are running unroped.

Islands in the Stream was published nine years after Hemingway's death, though he had begun it back in 1950. Set against the backdrop of World War II, it tells the story of a painter named Thomas Hudson, who comes to terms with the deaths of his three sons.

The Frozen Daiquiri has acquired something of a bad reputation, given that in the 1980s it became associated with sickeningly sweet, overly artificial drinks, but the original differs from an "ordinary" Daiquiri mainly in its use of crushed ice (the drink is mixed in a blender). It doesn't have to be especially sweet, and in fact, will be better if it's not.

Gin & Coconut Water

Islands in the Stream, Ernest Hemingway, 1970

1½ oz. gin

2 oz. coconut water

2 dashes of Angostura Bitters

1 strip of lemon peel, for garnish

Place the gin, coconut water, and bitters in a cocktail shaker, fill it two-thirds of the way with ice, and shake until chilled.

Strain over ice into a cocktail glass, garnish with the lemon peel, and enjoy.

Thomas Hudson took a sip of the ice-cold drink that tasted of the fresh green lime juice mixed with the tasteless coconut water that was still so much more full-bodied than any charged water, strong with the real Gordon's gin that made it alive to his tongue and rewarding to swallow, and all of it tautened by the bitters that gave it color.

In this scene, Hudson tries a drink unknown to him, as he is driven through an old neighborhood undergoing significant changes. In the manner you'd expect from a Hemingway antihero, he muses about how it's "a hell of a good drink." There are several variations on this mixed concoction, but his version calls for coconut water, Gordon's (or a gin of your choice), and bitters. Some recipes include ginger juice for a bit of extra kick.

Singapore Sling

Fear and Loathing in Las Vegas,
Hunter S. Thompson, 1971

1 oz. gin

1¾ tablespoons cherry brandy

2 teaspoons Cointreau

½ oz. Bénédictine

Dash of grenadine

1⅓ tablespoons fresh lime juice

1 oz. pineapple juice

Club soda, to top

Place all of the ingredients, except for the club soda, in a cocktail shaker, fill it two-thirds of the way with ice, and shake until chilled.

Strain over ice into a highball glass, top with club soda, and enjoy.

We had actually been sitting there in the Polo Lounge—for many hours—drinking Singapore Slings with mescal on the side and beer chasers. And when the call came, I was ready.

Thompson's classic, semiautobiographical novel vividly tells of a drug-fueled trip to Las Vegas taken by one Raoul Duke, and his attorney, Doctor Gonzo. The scene set in this excerpt happens just as the protagonist is about to get "the call" to go to Vegas, and he's already been knocking back Singapore Slings for some time.

The Singapore Sling actually did originate in Singapore, sometime in the early twentieth century. These days, the drink is often a fairly complex blend of ingredients, though originally, it consisted of gin, cherry liqueur, and the juices of lemon, lime, and orange. More recent versions often add in Grand Marnier and/or Bénédictine, as well as bitters.

Gin Fizz

Love in the Ruins, Walker Percy, 1971

1½ oz. gin

1 oz. fresh lemon juice

1 teaspoon simple syrup

1 egg white

Club soda, to top

Chill a Collins glass in the freezer.

Place all of the ingredients, except for the club soda, in a cocktail shaker and dry shake for 15 to 20 seconds. Fill the shaker one-quarter of the way with ice and shake for 3 to 5 minutes.

Pour the cocktail into a chilled Collins glass, top with club soda until a foamy head forms, and enjoy.

I've tossed off the whole drink somewhat nervously before it comes over me that it is a gin fizz. Oh well, I've got anti-allergy pills with me. The drink is deliciously cool and silky with albumen.

The Gin Fizz features prominently in Percy's speculative fiction about a future where the United States is fragmented along political and racial lines. Meant as a commentary on the upheavals of the 1960s, it seems as relevant now as ever. The main character, Dr. Thomas More, has invented a device that might help ease some social ills, but of course, there are those in the government who want to use it for their own purposes. Also, More is allergic to his favorite drink, and has to keep allergy pills on hand. Talk about a dystopia!

House of Lords Martini

Breakfast of Champions, Kurt Vonnegut, 1973

4 parts House of Lords gin
1 part dry vermouth
1 lemon twist, for garnish

Place the gin and vermouth in a mixing glass, fill it two-thirds of the way with ice, and stir until chilled.

Strain into a cocktail glass, garnish with the lemon twist, and enjoy.

I had her bring Dwayne Hoover his customary drink, which was a House of Lords martini with a twist of lemon peel.

Breakfast of Champions tells the tale of an encounter between two very different men, Kilgore Trout and Dwayne Hoover. Trout is a struggling science fiction writer, and Hoover is a successful businessman on the verge of going insane. After reading Trout's novel, Hoover finally loses his mind and the book details the violent rampage that ensues. Its surreal ending (involving time travel, among other things) makes it a mystifying read, though it's intended as a critique of the harsh nature of American society and its cruelty to its most vulnerable citizens.

The House of Lords Martini sounds very fancy, but it's really just a Martini made specifically with House of Lords gin, which is no longer produced, though there are some modern equivalents, such as the House of Lords gin from the Houses of Parliament shop in London. You'd probably have to time travel to get ahold of an original bottle.

Gin & Tonic

"Sympathy in White Major", Philip Larkin, 1974

2½ oz. gin

2½ oz. tonic water

Splash of fresh lime juice

1 lime wedge, for garnish

Fill a rocks glass with ice, add the gin and tonic water, and gently stir.

Top with the lime juice, garnish with the lime wedge, and enjoy.

When I drop four cubes of ice
Chimingly in a glass, and add
Three goes of gin, a lemon slice,
And let a ten-ounce tonic void
In foaming gulps until it smothers
Everything else up to the edge...

Larkin's short poem describes the making of a traditional Gin & Tonic. In subsequent stanzas, he raises his glass in a toast to an unnamed individual (possibly even himself), who seems to have gone out of his way to do things for others, and be kind and selfless. But in the end, he's not sure it did anyone any good. Is selflessness really all it's cracked up to be? The poem leaves us wondering.

The G & T is a classic of the cocktail world. At its simplest, it's a blend of gin, tonic water, and lime or lemon juice, poured over ice. It dates back to the early nineteenth century, possibly to the British colonial presence in India, where the quinine in tonic water was frequently used to treat malaria.

Stinger

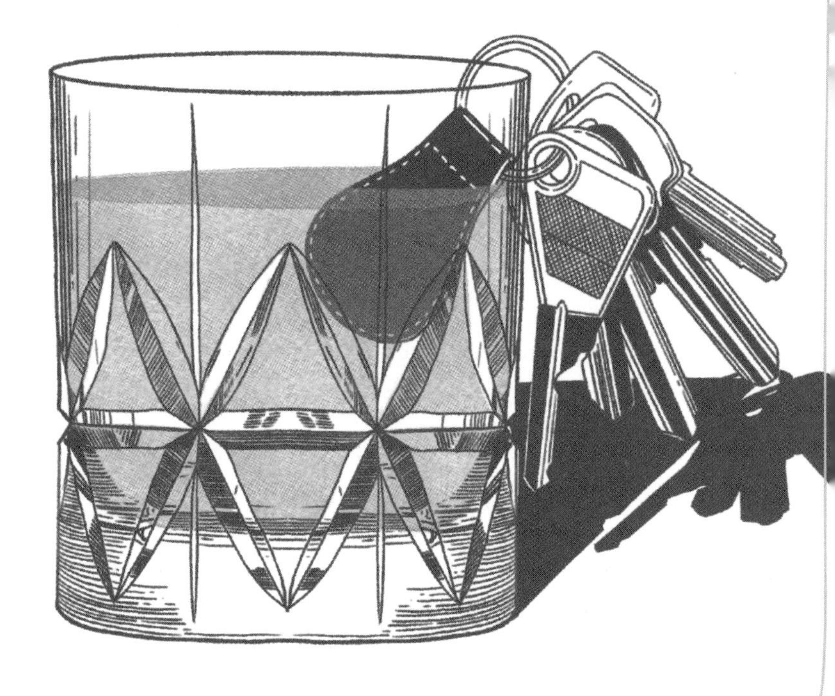

Rabbit Is Rich, John Updike, 1981

1 oz. brandy or cognac

½ oz crème de menthe

¼ oz. simple syrup (optional)

Chill a rocks glass in the freezer.

Place all of the ingredients in a cocktail shaker and dry shake for 10 to 15 seconds.

Add ice and shake until chilled.

Strain into the chilled rocks glass and enjoy.

Revitalized by food and their talk, they decide after all to sit with Stingers and watch the dancing a while, under the stars that on this night seem to Harry jewels of a clock that moves with maddening slowness.

Rabbit Is Rich is the third of Updike's Rabbit Angstrom books, set two decades after the first book. In this story, Rabbit and Janice are living comfortably, having inherited her father's car dealership and being in a much better financial position. But Rabbit remains unsatisfied about his life choices, and the Stinger is one of his consolations.

The Stinger is traditionally a two-ingredient cocktail, probably dating from the early 1890s. It is composed simply of brandy or cognac and crème de menthe. Some recipes call for simple syrup as well, but these two, most often served with ice, offer enough satisfaction, especially if you use a quality brandy.

Sweet Rob Roy

Hocus Pocus, Kurt Vonnegut, 1990

2 oz. Scotch whisky

1 oz. sweet vermouth

2 drops of Angostura Bitters

1 maraschino cherry, for garnish

Place the Scotch, vermouth, and bitters in a mixing glass, fill it two-thirds of the way with ice, and stir until chilled.

Strain into a cocktail glass, garnish with the maraschino cherry, and enjoy.

If I could order any drink I wanted now, it would be a Sweet Rob Roy on the Rocks, a Manhattan made with Scotch. That was another drink a woman introduced me to, and it made me laugh instead of cry, and fall in love with the woman who said to try one.

Vonnegut's experimental novel tells the tale of Eugene Debs Hartke, a Vietnam vet and teacher who gets in over his head while teaching at a segregated prison. He enjoys drinking a sweet version of the Rob Roy cocktail, only to find out that he has a son he never knew about. The son's name? Rob Roy.

The Rob Roy is made up mainly of Scotch and vermouth, and was invented in 1894 in New York, in honor of the premiere of the operetta *Rob Roy*, by Reginald De Koven, which is based on the life of the Scottish folk hero. The drink is "sweet" because it's made with sweet vermouth, and needs no additional ingredients, though dry versions exist, as well.

Berlin Station Chief

Harlot's Ghost, Norman Mailer, 1991

4 parts gin

1 part Scotch whisky

1 lemon twist, for garnish

Place the gin and Scotch in a mixing glass, fill it two-thirds of the way with ice, and stir until thoroughly combined.

Strain into a cocktail glass, garnish with the lemon twist, and enjoy.

He got up, went to the icebox, took out the makings, and mixed a batch of martinis: He filled his shaker with ice, poured in a quarter inch of Scotch, poured it out, then loaded the pitcher with gin. "The best Chicago hotels make it this way," he informed me.

Harlot's Ghost is a massive (well over 1,000 pages!) novel, a sprawling spy epic. It's an autobiography of its main character, Harry Hubbard, who details his exploits with the CIA in various tense situations around the world in the 1950s and 1960s. In this particular scene, Hubbard is introduced to a new cocktail—a Martini variation that substitutes Scotch for the vermouth. The drink might be Mailer's own invention, but some bartenders at the time of publication maintained that they'd been serving this mix for a while.

Use a single-malt Scotch, and if you like smoky flavors, go for one from Islay, which will provide a unique pairing with the herbaceous flavors of the gin. You might not be a globe-trotting spy, but you'll still appreciate the distinctive experience this drink provides.

Tequila Sunrise

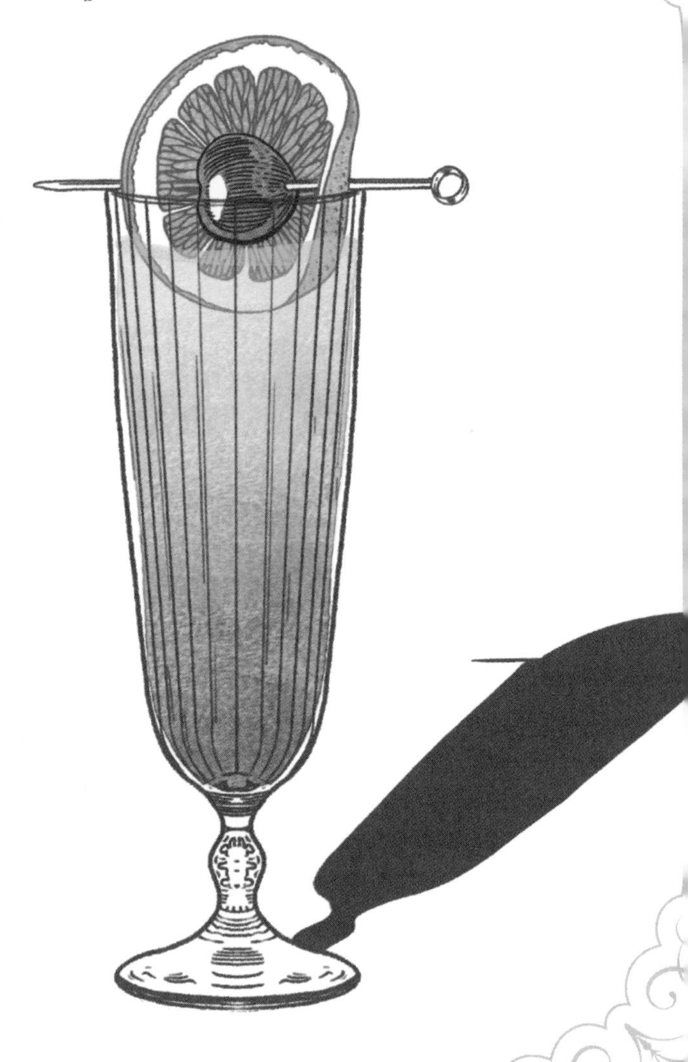

Bleeding Edge, Thomas Pynchon, 2013

2 oz. tequila

Dash of fresh lemon juice

4 oz. orange juice

Splash of grenadine

1 maraschino cherry, for garnish

1 orange slice, for garnish

Place the tequila and juices in a highball glass, fill it with ice, and stir until chilled.

Add the grenadine and do not stir; instead, let it filter down through the orange juice. Garnish with the maraschino cherry and orange slice and enjoy.

Train hostesses... keep coming by with carts full of junk food, drinks with Pacific subtexts like Tequila Sunrises...

Pynchon's novel is a surreal detective story with a truly modern flavor, involving conspiracies, hacking, and cybersecurity, as Maxine Tarnow investigates potential fraud at a security firm and finds that their numbers do not add up. And that's just the beginning.

The Tequila Sunrise dates back to the 1930s, though a modern version of the drink was invented in the 1970s at the Trident restaurant on Sausalito, California, and it's this version that is best known today. The name comes from its mix of tequila, orange juice, and grenadine. When the grenadine is added, it sinks to the bottom of the glass, giving the drink a beautiful layered look, rather like the sky when the sun rises. This beautiful drink can be enjoyed anytime, even if you're not trying to track down cyber criminals!

Your Favorite Writer's Favorite Drink

When they weren't writing drinks into their stories, many writers had their particular favorites, drinks that would either help them with the writing process, or hinder it, depending on the circumstances. The old adage of "write drunk, edit sober" probably held true for quite a few of them.

Caudle

William Shakespeare

1 egg

2 oz. wine

¾ oz. honey

2 sugar cubes

Dash of nutmeg or cinnamon, for garnish

Place the egg in a cocktail shaker and dry shake for 15 seconds.

Add the remaining ingredients, muddle, and add ice.

Shake until chilled and double-strain over ice into a Collins glass.

Garnish with nutmeg or cinnamon and enjoy.

To be perfectly honest, we don't know what Shakespeare's favorite drink was. Throughout his plays, a whole host of Tudor and Jacobean drinks feature: beer and ale, wine and sack, and more, and no doubt he indulged in all of them at one time or another. But the Caudle has been drunk since the Middle Ages in Europe. It is a blend of wine (or sometimes beer) with sugar or honey, eggs or egg yolks, and various spices according to taste, and heated. It was warming and satisfying, and thought to be especially good for the elderly, invalids, and new mothers. Undoubtedly, a Caudle or two would have been most welcome in the cold and rainy climate of England.

It's entirely possible that as the Bard toiled away on one of his many masterpieces, he had a Caudle close at hand for warmth and inspiration. This version is chilled, an update made for the modern palate.

Brandy Eggnog

Edgar Allan Poe

Dash of egg white
1 oz. simple syrup
1 oz. dark rum
1 oz. brandy
2 oz. warm milk
1 cinnamon stick, for garnish

Build the cocktail in a mug, adding the ingredients in the order they are listed.

Stir, garnish with the cinnamon stick, and enjoy.

For an early master of the macabre, Poe's drink of choice seems surprisingly festive and sweet: eggnog with brandy and often rum, too! He had a family recipe that included making his own nog, though if you want, you can simply substitute a store-bought version of eggnog during the holiday season. At any other time of the year, though, you'll need to whip up your own milky-eggy version to pour your spirits into. And of course, it was traditionally consumed warm to keep away winter's chill.

But even the finest of eggnogs won't keep away the chills induced by Poe's tales!

If you're skittish about the raw egg, heat the cocktail gently on the stove before pouring it into the mug. And if you're feeling lazy, you can replace the egg white and simple syrup with a bit of warmed, store-bought eggnog.

Apple Hot Toddy

Gustave Flaubert

1 teaspoon simple syrup

2 oz. calvados or applejack

½ apple, baked

½ oz. apricot brandy

½ oz. heavy cream

Boiling water, to top

Freshly grated nutmeg, for garnish

Place the syrup, calvados, baked apple, apricot brandy, and cream in a mug and top with the boiling water.

Gently stir, grate some nutmeg over the drink, and enjoy.

The author of *Madame Bovary* seems to have enjoyed a good drink or two, and might have endorsed one drink in particular, according to Alice B. Toklas, longtime partner of Gertrude Stein, and author of her own cookbook in 1954. This French winter drink might date to the eighteenth century, though Flaubert seems to have added his own spin to it.

The Apple Hot Toddy is a blend of Calvados (apple brandy), hard apple cider, apricot brandy, and heavy cream. Some versions omit the cider and just use the spirits and cream. Either way, this is a very northern French drink (it's said to come from Pont Audemer, near the mouth of the Seine in Normandy), and a most delicious one, suited to the colder months and perhaps sipping while reading a classic novel.

Whiskey Cock-Tail

Mark Twain

2 parts whiskey

1 part fresh lemon juice

Dash of Angostura Bitters

Pinch of caster (superfine) sugar

1 maraschino cherry, for garnish

Place the ingredients in a rocks glass, fill it with ice, and stir until chilled.

Garnish with the maraschino cherry.

In addition to writing about his drink-related frustrations in Paris (see pages 44 to 53), Twain had an affinity for his own version of a cocktail, one he first tasted abroad. He wrote to his wife: "Livy my darling, I want you to be sure and remember to have, in the bath-room, when I arrive, a bottle of Scotch whisky, a lemon, some crushed sugar, and a bottle of Angostura bitters. Ever since I have been in London I have taken in a wine glass what is called a cocktail (made with these ingredients) before breakfast, before dinner and before going to bed."

Twain's preferred drink is a Whiskey Sour without the egg white, which was apparently popular in London when he visited. This is a nice variation on the traditional drink, especially if you have an aversion to uncooked eggs in your drinks. Not that cooked eggs would be better, of course.

Clover Club

William Butler Yeats

5 raspberries, plus more for garnish

½ oz. simple syrup

1½ oz. London dry gin

½ oz. dry vermouth

½ oz. fresh lemon juice

½ oz. egg white

Place the raspberries and syrup in a cocktail shaker and muddle.

Add the remaining ingredients and dry shake for 20 seconds. Add ice and shake until chilled.

Strain into a coupe, skewer a few raspberries on a toothpick, garnish the cocktail with them, and enjoy.

Yeats seems an unlikely candidate for choosing a rather frivolous cocktail as one of his favorite drinks, but according to one story, it's absolutely true. The Clover Club cocktail was created at the Bellevue-Stratford Hotel bar in Philadelphia, and meant as something of a joke: made to be consumed by "serious gentlemen" who met once a month to let their proverbial hair down and mock one another in good fun.

When Yeats tried one at a lunch in his honor, he was at first suspicious, of course, but according to a journalist at the event: "Yeats tasted the cocktail, and smacked his lips. Another taste. His eye gleamed and his face lighted up. But, to the surprise of his hosts, he declined to gulp. This thing must be taken slowly. It was filled with a variety of flavors, and it must be tasted all the way down to the bottom of the glass. So he just sat and sipped that Clover Club Cocktail. When wine was brought and proffered him, he waved it away. 'Another of the same,' he said, in effect, and he kept sipping Clover Club Cocktails all the way through the meal."

Horse's Neck

Jack London

2½ oz. rye whiskey

1 oz. ginger ale

1 oz. fresh lemon juice

1 maraschino cherry, for garnish

1 lemon slice, for garnish

Place the whiskey, ginger ale, and lemon juice in a cocktail shaker, fill it two-thirds of the way with ice, and shake until chilled.

Strain over ice into a highball glass, garnish with the maraschino cherry and lemon slice, and enjoy.

London is, of course, known for books such as *Call of the Wild* and *White Fang.* He also enjoyed this simple mix, which dates back to the later nineteenth century. It's simply a blend of whiskey or brandy with ginger ale. Optional additions include lemon juice and/or some bitters, but they're not essential.

Like a number of writers, London seemed to enjoy this and other drinks far too much, and alcoholism eventually ruined his immense talent.

Hot Toddy

William Faulkner

1 oz. bourbon

1 tablespoon honey

2 teaspoons fresh lemon juice

½ cup boiling water

1 lemon wedge, for garnish

1 cinnamon stick, for garnish

Place the bourbon, honey, and lemon juice in a mug, pour the boiling water over the top, and stir to combine.

Garnish with the lemon wedge and cinnamon stick and enjoy.

Faulkner is famous for his novels and short stories set in the fictional Yoknapatawpha County in Mississippi, and his works earned him a Nobel Prize in 1949. He loved many different kinds of drinks (often to excess), including the Mint Julep. But he also had a fondness for the Hot Toddy, a classic winter warmer that has long been praised for its medicinal value.

There are many variations on the Hot Toddy, but it usually contains bourbon, hot water, honey, and lemon. Black tea, ginger, and other assorted ingredients can also be added in, according to taste. It's especially nice on a cold winter night, or when feeling unwell, and can be a good send-off to restful sleep.

Pompier

E.B. White

4 parts gin

1 part fresh lime juice

1 part apricot brandy

1 part dry vermouth

Honey syrup, to taste

Place the gin, lime juice, brandy, and vermouth in a highball glass, fill it with ice, and stir until chilled.

Add honey syrup to taste, stir to incorporate, and enjoy.

White is the author of the beloved children's books, *Charlotte's Web* and *Stuart Little*, as well as that famed resource for writers, *Elements of Style*. But it's his contribution to the world of cocktails that concerns us here. He devised the Pompier, his own variation on the Martini, and left detailed instructions in 1979 on how to prepare it:

"Equal parts lime juice, apricot brandy, honey, and dry vermouth. Stir this all together (you only need a tiny amount of the whole business), then add 4 times the amount of gin. Plenty of ice, stir, and serve."

The combination of both apricot brandy and honey will make this drink quite sweet, so you might want to adjust the amount of each to suit your taste.

Death in the Afternoon

Ernest Hemingway

1 oz. absinthe *Champagne, chilled, to top*

In a cocktail book from 1935, Hemingway offered up his own instructions for how to make it:

"Pour one jigger absinthe into a Champagne glass. Add iced Champagne until it attains the proper opalescent milkiness. Drink three to five of these slowly." All right, then!

Hemingway loved many different drinks, of course—especially Daiquiris—but the morbidly named Death in the Afternoon was one of his own inventions, being a blend of absinthe and Champagne. It also shares the name with his 1932 nonfiction book about Spanish bullfighting.

Spiked Lemonade

Zelda Fitzgerald

1 part vodka
4 parts lemonade
1 lemon slice, for garnish
1 fresh mint leaf, for garnish

Fill a highball glass with ice.

Add the vodka and lemonade and stir until chilled.

Garnish with the lemon slice and mint leaf and enjoy.

Wife of F. Scott Fitzgerald, and an accomplished author in her own right, Zelda Fitzgerald was known for wholeheartedly embracing the glamorous lifestyle of the 1920s. Prohibition meant nothing to her, of course, and she always made sure to keep connections with various bootleggers to keep herself, her husband, and their guests in all the alcohol they required, even if it meant doing without some other necessities.

One of Zelda's favorite alcoholic concoctions was simply to mix spirits with some kind of fruit juice, and she was especially fond of Vodka Lemonade, a refreshing blend that makes for an excellent summer drink. Use a quality vodka and a lemonade made with freshly squeezed lemons (store-bought is fine, but look for the highest-quality offering you can get). A garnish of mint adds the perfect topping!

Ramos Gin Fizz

Tennessee Williams

2 oz. gin

1 oz. half-and-half

¾ oz. simple syrup

½ oz. fresh lemon juice

½ oz. fresh lime juice

2 dashes of orange blossom water

1 egg white

Club soda, to top

Chill a Collins glass in the freezer.

Place all of the ingredients, except for the club soda, in a cocktail shaker and dry shake for 15 to 20 seconds.

Fill the shaker one-quarter of the way with ice and shake for 3 to 5 minutes.

Pour the cocktail into the chilled Collins glass, top with club soda until a foamy head forms, and enjoy.

The famed writer of *Cat on a Hot Tin Roof* had his characters in that play knocking back much bourbon over the course of an evening, but in his personal life, he seems to have been fond of the Ramos Gin Fizz, which dates back to 1888 in New Orleans, and is a classic Southern drink. *Esquire* magazine once noted: "If the Sidecar is jazz, the Ramos Fizz is ragtime."

It can be distinguished from the standard Gin Fizz by the addition of dairy and orange blossom water, which add new levels of flavor and texture to the traditional drink.

Vodka & Coke

William S. Burroughs

1 oz. vodka
4 oz. Coca-Cola
1 lemon or lime wedge, for garnish

Place the vodka and Coca-Cola in a highball glass, fill it with ice, and stir until chilled.

Garnish with lemon or lime wedge and enjoy.

Burroughs is best known for his surreal novel, *The Naked Lunch*, and he was a leading voice of the Beat Generation. As he grew older, he came to value a daily Vodka & Coke, and would mix one promptly at 6:00 pm each day. So fond of vodka was he that he even entertained the idea of Absolut Vodka producing an ad using some of his artwork, and calling it "Absolute Burroughs," but it never came to be.

This simple blend of vodka and Coca-Cola is a variation on the Rum & Coke, and is easy to make. It requires nothing else but these two ingredients, poured over ice if you wish, though you could also add a lime wedge for color and garnish. Some recipes also call for the addition of bitters to make the flavor a bit more complex.

Sonnie Boy

Carson McCullers

1 part dry sherry

2 parts freshly brewed tea

1 lemon wedge, for garnish

Place the sherry and tea in a mug and stir to combine.

Garnish with the lemon wedge and enjoy.

McCullers wrote novels, short stories, plays, and more, work that often explored the place of outsiders in the American South, and can be considered part of the Southern Gothic genre. She was especially fond of a drink she called the Sonnie Boy, which was a simple mixture of hot tea and sherry. She would keep this in a thermos and drink it throughout the day when writing, sometimes claiming it was "just" tea.

The Sonnie Boy would make a nice, simple alternative to a Hot Toddy. Use whatever tea you like—black, green, herbal—and a dry sherry, added to taste, but be realistic! A lemon wedge and honey are optional, but nice extras.

Boilermaker

Charles Bukowski

1 (12 oz.) can of beer *1 oz. whiskey*

Pour the beer into a pint glass and pour the whiskey into a shot glass. Drop the shot glass into the beer and drink immediately.

Bukowski was a poet and novelist who wrote about many of the key social issues of the day, so much so that his controversial takes in an underground newspaper led to the FBI keeping a file on him. He was notoriously fond of alcohol, once saying: "That's the problem with drinking, I thought, as I poured myself a drink. If something bad happens you drink in an attempt to forget; if something good happens you drink in order to celebrate; and if nothing happens you drink to make something happen."

One of his drinks of choice was the Boilermaker, which is quite simple and to the point: it's whiskey and beer. Preferably a lot more beer than whiskey (bourbon will do nicely for the latter). The traditional way of making it is a bit odd, though: you fill your glass halfway with beer, fill a shot glass with whiskey, and then drop the shot glass into the beer glass! Note that this is in no way required, and you can simply pour in the whiskey—or even enjoy it on the side.

Margarita

Jack Kerouac

Salt, for the rim

2 oz. tequila

1 oz. orange liqueur

1 oz. fresh lime juice

1 lime wheel, for garnish

Wet the rim of a coupe and coat it with salt. If desired, add ice to the glass.

Place the tequila, orange liqueur, and lime juice in a cocktail shaker, fill it two-thirds of the way with ice, and shake until chilled.

Strain into the rimmed glass, garnish with the lime wheel, and enjoy.

Kerouac traveled widely and was a key voice for the Beat Generation, writing books such as *On the Road* and *Big Sur.* He also spent time in Mexico, and it's possible that while there, he developed his liking for the classic Margarita, a drink so common now that in the United States many can scarcely imagine a Mexican meal without one.

Though the drink's origins are unclear (a common problem in the cocktail world), the traditional Margarita is made up of tequila, triple sec (orange liqueur), and lime juice, with the obligatory salt on the glass. Add in some ice and you have a perfect drink for enjoying on a hot day, a welcome relief from the toil of one's travels.

Screwdriver

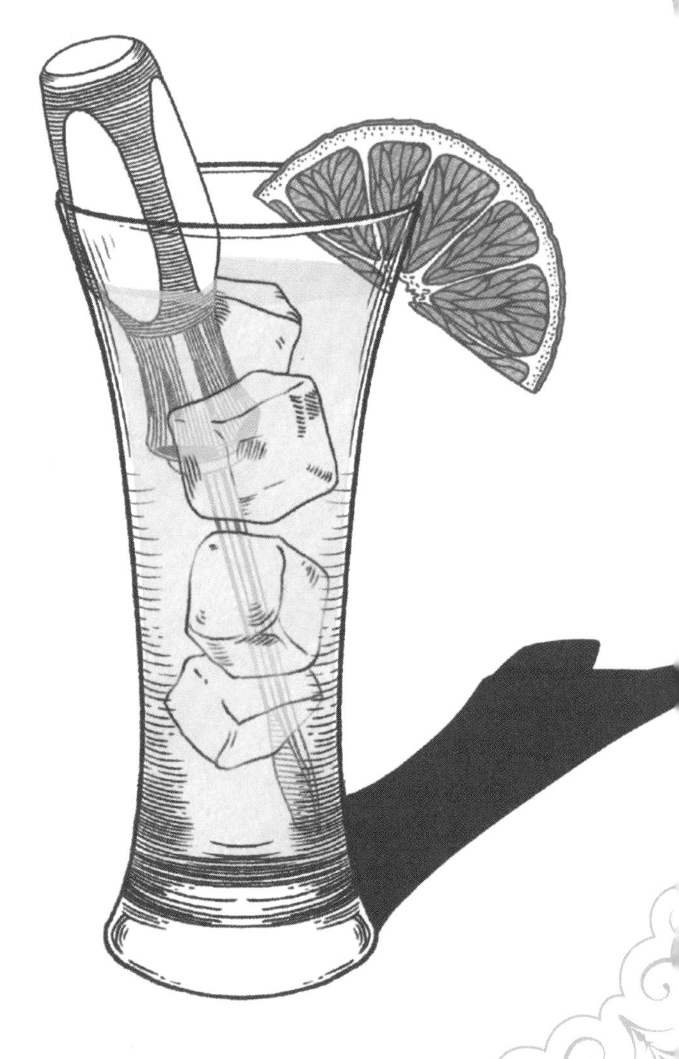

Truman Capote

2 oz. vodka

4 oz. orange juice

1 orange slice, for garnish

Fill a highball glass with ice, add the vodka, and top with the orange juice.

Stir until chilled, garnish with the orange slice, and enjoy.

A master of the true crime and Southern Gothic genres, Capote loved his mixed drinks and loved to socialize with others while downing them. Among his favorites was the "orange thingee," a simple mix of vodka and orange juice, commonly called a Screwdriver.

One story about its origins suggests that it was invented by workers in the Persian Gulf, who would secretly add vodka to their orange juice. Since they didn't have spoons to stir with, they used screwdrivers. Yeah, it's probably not true, but it's a good story. In any case, this simple drink really wants and needs nothing else, except ice, and even that isn't essential.

Vodka Tonic

Salman Rushdie

1 oz. vodka

4 oz. tonic water

1 lemon or lime wedge, for garnish

Fill a highball glass with ice, add the vodka and tonic, and stir until chilled.

Garnish with the lemon or lime wedge and enjoy.

Rushdie is an author who is no stranger to controversy, from having to go into hiding after death threats for his 1988 novel, *The Satanic Verses*, to his recent woes from being attacked and seriously injured by an extremist. Through it all, he has maintained a good attitude and a commitment to his highly innovative work.

In various interviews he has spoken of his liking for a simple drink, the Vodka Tonic. Served in a highball glass, it's a combination of vodka and tonic water in whatever proportions you prefer, and you can also add ice and a wedge of lemon or lime to complete the flavor profile.

Cosmopolitan

Candice Bushnell

1 oz. vodka

1 oz. triple sec

1½ oz. cranberry juice

½ oz. fresh lime juice

1 lime wheel, for garnish

Chill a cocktail glass in the freezer.

Place the vodka, triple sec, cranberry juice, and lime juice in a cocktail shaker, fill it two-thirds of the way with ice, and shake until chilled.

Strain into the chilled glass, garnish with the lime wheel, and enjoy.

Bushnell was the author of a 1990s column for *The New York Observer* that became the basis for the wildly popular television series, *Sex and the City*. She's also written a number of novels, some of which have also been adapted for television.

Bushnell is, by her own admission, quite fond of the Cosmopolitan, and has even posted her method for making her "Belvedere Cosmo" on her Instagram page. The Cosmo is a tasty combination of vodka, an orange liqueur (such as triple sec), cranberry juice, and lime juice, shaken with ice and poured into a glass. A garnish of a lime and/or skewered fruits makes for a nice-looking, delicious drink.

Metric Conversions

US Measurement	Approximate Metric Liquid Measurement	Approximate Metric Dry Measurement
1 teaspoon	5 ml	5 g
1 tablespoon or ½ ounce	15 ml	14 g
1 ounce or ⅛ cup	30 ml	29 g
¼ cup or 2 ounces	60 ml	57 g
⅓ cup	80 ml	76 g
½ cup or 4 ounces	120 ml	113 g
⅔ cup	160 ml	151 g
¾ cup or 6 ounces	180 ml	170 g
1 cup or 8 ounces or ½ pint	240 ml	227 g
1½ cups or 12 ounces	350 ml	340 g
2 cups or 1 pint or 16 ounces	475 ml	454 g
3 cups or 1½ pints	700 ml	680 g
4 cups or 2 pints or 1 quart	950 ml	908 g

Index